A Global Ethic

A Global Ethic

The Declaration of the Parliament of the World's Religions

Edited by Hans Küng and
Karl-Josef Kuschel

CONTINUUM • NEW YORK

1993

The Continuum Publishing Company
370 Lexington Avenue
New York, NY 10017

Translation of the German texts by John Bowden from
*Erklärung zum Weltethos. Die Deklaration des Parlamentes der
Weltreligionen*, published 1993 by R. Piper GmbH & Co KG,
Munich.

Printed in the United States of America

ISBN 0-8264-0640-8

Library of Congress Catalog Card Number 93-073808

Contents

Preface   7

The Parliament of the World's Religions
Declaration Toward a Global Ethic   11

Introduction   13

The Principles of a Global Ethic   17

I. No new global order without a new global
ethic   18

II. A fundamental demand: Every human
being must be treated humanely   21

III. Four irrevocable directives   24

    1. Commitment to a culture of non-violence
      and respect for life   24

    2. Commitment to a culture of solidarity
      and a just economic order   26

    3. Commitment to a culture of tolerance and
      a life of truthfulness   29

    4. Commitment to a culture of equal rights and
      partnership between men and women   32

IV. A transformation of consciousness   34

Commentaries and Background   41

Hans Küng

The History, Significance and Method of the Declaration Toward a Global Ethic   43

1. The prehistory   45

2. The preparations for the text   49

3. What had to be avoided in a declaration
   on a global ethic   53

4. What a declaration on a global ethic should
   contain   58

5. In the name of God? The Buddhists' objection   61

6. Disputed questions   65

7. A sign of hope   72

Karl-Josef Kuschel

The Parliament of the World's Religions, 1893-1993   77

1. How it all began   78

2. What is a 'parliament' of religions?   80

3. A latent 'Anglo-Saxon triumphalism'?   82

4. The collapse of Eurocentric Christian
   modernity   86

5. The polyreligious situation of our time:
   Chicago as an example   91

6. Conflicts and opportunities in the 1993
   Parliament   94

7. The main themes: Global thinking -
   spirituality - ethics   97

Documentation 107

A. The Opening Plenary of the Parliament 109

I. Procession of the Delegations   109

II. The Ceremony   119

B. The Closing Plenary of the Parliament 122

I. Procession of the Delegations   122

II. The Ceremony   123

Preface

Today, no one can still have any serious doubts that a period of the world which has been shaped more than any before it by world politics, world technology, the world economy and world civilization, needs a world ethic. That means a **fundamental consensus** concerning binding values, irrevocable standards, and personal attitudes. Without a basic consensus over ethics any society is threatened sooner or later by chaos or a dictatorship. There can be no better global order without a global ethic.

Here a global ethic means neither a global ideology, nor a single unified global religion transcending all existing religions, nor a mixture of all religions. Humanity is weary of unified ideologies, and in any case the religions of the world are so different in their views of faith and 'dogmas', their symbols and rites, that a 'unification' of them would be meaningless, a distasteful syncretistic cocktail.

Nor does a global ethic seek to replace the high ethics of the individual religions with an ethical minimalism. The Torah of the Jews, the Christians' Sermon on the Mount, the Muslims' Qur'an, the Hindus' Bhagavadgita, the Discourses of the Buddha, the Sayings of Confucius - for hundreds and millions of men and women all these remain the foundation for faith and life, thought and action. What then?

A global ethic seeks to work out what is already common to the religions of the world now despite all

7

their differences over human conduct, moral values and basic moral convictions. In other words, a global ethic does not reduce the religions to an ethical minimalism but represents the minimum of **what the religions of the world already have in common now in the ethical sphere.** It is not directed against anyone, but invites all, believers and non-believers, to make this ethic their own and act in accordance with it.

For the first time in the history of religions, the Council of the Parliament of the World's Religions, which met in Chicago from 28 August to 4 September 1993, and in which 6,500 people from every possible religion took part, ventured to work out and present a 'Declaration Toward a Global Ethic'. As was only to be expected, this declaration provoked vigorous discussion during the Parliament. However, the welcome thing is that at a time when so many religions are entangled in political conflicts, indeed in bloody wars, representatives of very different religions, great and small, endorsed this Declaration with their signatures on behalf of countless believers on this earth.

This Declaration now forms the basis for an extensive process of discussion and acceptance which we hope will be sparked off in all religions. For of course this Declaration Toward a Global Ethic - like the first Declaration on Human Rights in 1776 at the time of the American Revolution - is not an end but a beginning. That was clear from the start, and it was expressed clearly again at the end of the Parliament when this declaration was termed an 'Initial Declaration Toward a Global Ethic'. The hope is that this document may set off a process which changes the behaviour of men and women in the religions in the direction of understanding, respect and cooperation. And if all goes well, in the not too distant future we shall have other declarations which make the global ethic of the religions more precise and concrete and add further illustrations to it. Perhaps one day there may even be a United Nations Declaration on a Global Ethic to provide moral support for the Declaration on Human Rights, which is so often ignored and cruelly violated.

But is not such an expectation sheer illusion? Can the religions be expected to accept such a declaration? Are such hopes realistic? To the eternal sceptics and pessimists we would say: No one will deny that within the space of two or three decades it has proved possible to bring about worldwide a universal change of awareness about economics and ecology, about world peace and disarmament, and about the partnership between men and women. Our document here has been written and approved in the hope that a similar change of awareness may take place over a basic ethic common to all humankind, a global ethic. It is up to the religions of this earth and to people all over the world, in a quite practical way, wherever they are, to make sure that this Declaration remains more than paper, that it is filled with life, that it inspires people to a life of mutual respect, understanding and cooperation.

This Preface cannot end without a warm word of thanks to those who organized the Parliament of the World Religions in Chicago, especially Dr David Ramage, Chairperson of the Board of Trustees, Dr Daniel Gómez-Ibáñez, Executive Director, and all the many selfless, efficient, and friendly helpers who in preparing for and seeing through the Parliament of the World's

Religions coped with an enormous burden of work in an admirable way.

Chicago/Tübingen, September 1993

Hans Küng
Karl-Josef Kuschel

The Parliament of the World's Religions

Declaration Toward a Global Ethic

*The text entitled 'Introduction' was produced by an Editorial Committee of the 'Council' of the Parliament of the World's Religions in Chicago on the basis of the Declaration composed in Tübingen (here headed 'Principles'). It was meant to serve as a brief summary of the Declaration for publicity purposes. At the same time it was intended to be read aloud in public. So this text was read out publicly at the solemn concluding plenary on 4 September 1993 in Grant Park, Chicago: a number of passages were greeted with spontaneous applause by the audience of thousands.

Introduction*

The world is in agony. The agony is so pervasive and urgent that we are compelled to name its manifestations so that the depth of this pain may be made clear.

Peace eludes us ... the planet is being destroyed ... neighbours live in fear ... women and men are estranged from each other ... children die!

This is abhorrent!

We condemn the abuses of Earth's ecosystems.

We condemn the poverty that stifles life's potential; the hunger that weakens the human body; the economic disparities that threaten so many families with ruin.

We condemn the social disarray of the nations; the disregard for justice which pushes citizens to the margin; the anarchy overtaking our communities; and the insane death of children from violence. In particular we condemn aggression and hatred in the name of religion.

But this agony need not be.

It need not be because the basis for an ethic already exists. This ethic offers the possibility of a better individual and global order, *and leads individuals away from despair and societies away from chaos.*

We are women and men who have embraced the precepts and practices of the world's religions.

We affirm that a common set of core values is found in the teachings of the religions, and that these form the basis of a global ethic.

We affirm that this truth is already known, but yet to be lived in heart and action.

We affirm that there is an irrevocable, unconditional norm for all areas of life, for families and communities, for races, nations and religions. There already exist ancient guidelines for human behaviour which are found in the teachings of the religions of the world and which are the conditions for a sustainable world order.

We declare:

We are interdependent. Each of us depends on the well-being of the whole, and so we have respect for the community of living beings, for people, animals, and plants, and for the preservation of Earth, the air, water and soil.

We take individual responsibility for all we do. All our decisions, actions, and failures to act have consequences.

We must treat others as we wish others to treat us. We make a commitment to respect life and dignity, individuality and diversity, so that every person is treated humanely, without exception. We must have patience and acceptance. We must be able to forgive, learning from the past but never allowing ourselves to be enslaved by memories of hate. Opening our hearts to one another, we must sink our narrow differences for the cause of world community, practising a culture of solidarity and relatedness.

We consider humankind our family. We must strive to be kind and generous. We must not live for ourselves alone, but should also serve others, never forgetting the children, the aged, the poor, the suffering, the disabled, the refugees, and the lonely. No person should ever be considered or treated as a second-class citizen, or be exploited in any way whatsoever. There should be equal partnership between men and women. We must not commit any kind of sexual immorality. We must put behind us all forms of domination or abuse.

We commit ourselves to a culture of non-violence, respect, justice and peace. We shall not oppress, injure, torture, or kill other human beings, forsaking violence as a means of settling differences.

We must strive for a just social and economic order, in which everyone has an equal chance to reach full potential as a human being. We must speak and act truthfully and with compassion, dealing fairly with all, and avoiding prejudice and hatred. We must not steal. We must move beyond the dominance of greed for power, prestige, money, and consumption to make a just and peaceful world. Earth cannot be changed for the better unless the consciousness of individuals is changed first. We pledge to increase our awareness by disciplining our minds, by meditation, by prayer, or by positive thinking. Without risk and a readiness to sacrifice there can be no fundamental change in our situation. Therefore we commit ourselves to this global ethic, to understanding one another, and to socially-beneficial, peace-fostering, and nature-friendly ways of life.

We invite all people, whether religious or not, to do the same.

The Principles of a Global Ethic

Our world is experiencing a **fundamental crisis:** a crisis in global economy, global ecology, and global politics. The lack of a grand vision, the tangle of unresolved problems, political paralysis, mediocre political leadership with little insight or foresight, and in general too little sense for the commonweal are seen everywhere. Too many old answers to new challenges.

Hundreds of millions of human beings on our planet increasingly suffer from unemployment, poverty, hunger, and the destruction of their families. Hope for a lasting peace among nations slips away from us. There are tensions between the sexes and generations. Children die, kill, and are killed. More and more countries are shaken by corruption in politics and business. It is increasingly difficult to live together peacefully in our cities because of social, racial, and ethnic conflicts, the abuse of drugs, organized crime, and even anarchy. Even neighbours often live in fear of one another. Our planet continues to be ruthlessly plundered. A collapse of the ecosystem threatens us.

Time and again we see leaders and members of **religions** incite aggression, fanaticism, hate, and xenophobia - even inspire and legitimate violent and bloody conflicts. Religion often is misused for purely power-political goals, including war. We are filled with disgust.

We condemn these blights and declare that they need not be. An ethic already exists within the religious teachings of the world which can counter the global distress. Of course this ethic provides no direct solution for all the immense problems of the world, but it does supply the moral foundation for a better individual and global order: a **vision** which can lead women and men away from despair, and society away from chaos.

We are persons who have committed ourselves to the precepts and practices of the world's religions. We confirm that there is already a consensus among the religions which can be the basis for a global ethic - a minimal **fundamental consensus** concerning binding **values**, irrevocable **standards**, and fundamental **moral attitudes**.

I. No new global order without a new global ethic

We women and men of various religions and regions of Earth therefore address all people, religious and non-religious. We wish to express the following convictions which we hold in common.

- We **all** have a **responsibility for a better global order**.

- Our involvement for the sake of human rights, freedom, justice, peace, and the preservation of Earth is absolutely necessary.

- Our different religious and cultural traditions must not prevent our common involvement in opposing all forms of inhumanity and working for greater humaneness.

- The principles expressed in this global ethic can be affirmed by all persons with ethical convictions, whether religiously grounded or not.

As **religious and spiritual persons** we base our lives on an Ultimate Reality, and draw spiritual power and hope therefrom, in trust, in prayer or meditation, in word or silence. We have a special responsibility for the welfare of all humanity and care for the planet Earth. We do not consider ourselves better than other women and men, but we trust that the ancient wisdom of our religions can point the way for the future.

After two world wars and the end of the cold war, the collapse of fascism and nazism, the shaking to the foundations of communism and colonialism, humanity has entered a new phase of its history. Today we possess sufficient economic, cultural, and spiritual resources to introduce a better global order, but old and new **ethnic, national, social, economic, and religious tensions** threaten the peaceful building of a better world. We have experienced greater technological progress than ever before, yet we see that world-wide poverty, hunger, death of children, unemployment, misery, and the destruction of nature have not diminished but rather have increased. Many peoples are threatened with economic ruin, social disarray, political marginalization, ecological catastrophe, and moral collapse.

In such a dramatic global situation humanity needs a **vision of peoples living peacefully together,** of ethnic and ethical groupings and of religions sharing responsibility for the care of Earth. A vision rests on hopes, goals, ideals, standards. But all over the world these have slipped from our hands. Yet we are convinced that, despite their frequent abuses and failures, it is the communities of faith who bear a responsibility to demonstrate that such hopes, ideals, and standards can be guarded, grounded and lived. This is especially true in the modern state. Guarantees of freedom of conscience and religion are necessary, but they do not substitute for binding values, convictions, and norms which are valid for all humans regardless of their social origin, sex, skin colour, language, or religion.

We are convinced of the fundamental unity of the human family on Earth. We recall the 1948 Universal Declaration of Human Rights of the United Nations. What it formally proclaimed on the level of **rights** we wish to confirm and deepen here from the perspective of an **ethic:** the full realization of the intrinsic dignity of the human person, the inalienable freedom and equality in principle of all humans, and the necessary solidarity and interdependence of all humans with each other.

On the basis of personal experiences and the burden-some history of our planet we have learned

- that a better global order cannot be created or enforced by laws, prescriptions, and conventions alone;

- that the realization of peace, justice, and the protection of earth depends on the insight and readiness of men and women to act justly;

- that action in favour of rights and freedoms presumes a consciousness of responsibility and duty, and that therefore both the minds and hearts of women and men must be addressed;

- that rights without morality cannot long endure, and that there will be **no better global order without a global ethic.**

By a global ethic we do not mean a global ideology or **a single unified religion** beyond all existing religions, and certainly not the domination of one religion over all others. By a global ethic we mean a **fundamental consensus on binding values, irrevocable standards, and personal attitudes.** Without such a fundamental consensus on an ethic, sooner or later every community will be threatened by chaos or dictatorship, and individuals will despair.

II. A fundamental demand: Every human being must be treated humanely

We all are fallible, imperfect men and women with limitations and defects. We know the reality of evil. Precisely because of this, we feel compelled for the sake of global welfare to express what the fundamental elements of a global ethic should be - for individuals as well as for communities and organizations, for states as well as for the religions themselves. We trust that our often millennia-old religious and ethical traditions provide an ethic which is convincing and practical for **all women and men of good will,** religious and non-religious.

At the same time we know that our various religious and ethical traditions often offer very different bases of what is helpful and what is unhelpful for men and women, what is right and what is wrong, what is good and what is evil. We do not wish to gloss over or ignore the serious differences among the individual religions. However, they should not hinder us from proclaiming publicly **those things which we already hold in common** and which we jointly affirm, each on the basis of our own religious or ethical grounds.

We know that religions cannot solve the environmental, economic, political, and social problems of Earth. However, they can provide what obviously cannot be attained by economic plans, political programmes or legal regulations alone: **a change in** the inner orientation, the whole mentality, **the 'hearts' of people**, and a conversion from a false path to a new orientation for life. Humankind urgently needs social and ecological reforms, but it needs **spiritual renewal** just as urgently. As religious or spiritual persons we commit ourselves to this task. The spiritual powers of the religions can offer a fundamental sense of trust, a ground of meaning, ultimate standards, and a spiritual home. Of course religions are credible only when they eliminate those conflicts which spring from the religions themselves, dismantling mutual arrogance, mistrust, prejudice, and even hostile images, and thus demonstrate respect for the traditions, holy places, feasts, and rituals of people who believe differently.

Now as before, **women and men are treated inhumanely** all over the world. They are robbed of their opportunities and their freedom; their human rights are trampled underfoot; their dignity is disregarded. But might does not make right! In the face of all humanity our religious and ethical convictions demand that **every human being must be treated humanely!**

This means that every human being without distinction of age, sex, race, skin colour, physical or mental ability, language, religion, political view, or national or social origin possesses an inalienable and **untouchable dignity.** And everyone, the individual as well as the state, is therefore obliged to honour this dignity and protect it. Humans must always be the subjects of rights, must be ends, never mere means, never objects of commercialization and industrialization in economics, politics and media, in research institutes, and industrial corporations. No one stands 'above good and evil' - no human being, no social class, no influential interest group, no cartel, no police apparatus, no army, and no state. On the contrary; possessed of reason and conscience, every human is obliged to behave in a genuinely human fashion, to **do good and avoid evil!**

It is the intention of this Global Ethic to clarify what this means. In it we wish to recall irrevocable, unconditional ethical norms. These should not be bonds and chains, but helps and supports for people to find and realize once again their lives' directions, orientations, and meaning.

There is a principle which is found and has persisted in many religious and ethical traditions of humankind for thousands of years: **What you do not wish done to yourself, do not do to others!** Or in positive terms: **What you wish done to yourself, do to others!** This should be the irrevocable, unconditional norm for all areas of life, for families and communities, for races, nations and religions.

Every form of egoism should be rejected: all selfishness, whether individual or collective, whether in the form of class thinking, racism, nationalism, or sexism. We condemn these because they prevent humans from being authentically human. Self-determination and self-realization are thoroughly legitimate so long as they are not separated from human self-responsibility and global responsibility, that is, from reponsibility for fellow humans and for the planet Earth.

This principle implies very concrete standards to which we humans should hold firm. From it arise **four broad, ancient guidelines** for human behaviour which are found in most of the religions of the world.

III. Four irrevocable directives

1. Commitment to a culture of non-violence and respect for life

Numberless women and men of all regions and religions strive to lead lives not determined by egoism but by commitment to their fellow humans and to the world around them. Nevertheless, all over the world we find endless hatred, envy, jealousy and violence, not only between individuals but also between social and ethnic groups, between classes, races, nations, and religions. The use of violence, drug trafficking and organized crime, often equipped with new technical possibilities, has reached global proportions. Many places are still ruled by terror 'from above'; dictators oppress their own people, and institutional violence is widespread. Even in some countries where laws exist to protect individual freedoms, prisoners are tortured, men and women are mutilated, hostages are killed.

(a) In the great ancient religious and ethical traditions of humankind we find the directive: **You shall not kill!** Or in positive terms: **Have respect for life!** Let us reflect anew on the consequences of this ancient directive: all people have a right to life, safety, and the free development of personality in so far as they do not injure the rights of others. No one has the right physically or psychically to torture, injure, much less kill, any other human being. And no people, no state, no race, no religion has the right to hate, to discriminate against, to 'cleanse', to exile, much less to liquidate a 'foreign' minority which is different in behaviour or holds different beliefs.

(b) Of course, wherever there are humans there will be conflicts. Such conflicts, however, should be resolved without violence within a framework of justice. This is true for states as well as for individuals. Persons who hold political power must work within the framework of a just order and commit themselves to the most non-violent, peaceful solutions possible. And they should work for this within an international order of peace which itself has need of protection and defence against perpetrators of violence. Armament is a mistaken path; disarmament is the commandment of the times. Let no one be deceived: There is no survival for humanity without global peace!

(c) Young people must learn at home and in school that violence may not be a means of settling differences with others. Only thus can a **culture of non-violence be created**.

(d) A human person is infinitely precious and must be unconditionally protected. But likewise the **lives of animals and plants** which inhabit this planet with us deserve protection, preservation, and care. Limitless exploitation of the natural foundations of life, ruthless destruction of the biosphere, and militarization of the cosmos are all outrages. As human beings we have a special responsibility - especially with a view to future generations - for Earth and the cosmos, for the air, water, and soil. We are **all intertwined together** in this cosmos and we are all dependent on each other. Each one of us depends on the welfare of all. Therefore the dominance of humanity over nature and the cosmos must not be encouraged. Instead we must cultivate living in harmony with nature and the cosmos.

(e) To be authentically human in the spirit of our great religious and ethical traditions means that in public as well as in private life we must be concerned for others and ready to help. We must never be ruthless and brutal. Every people, every race, every religion must show tolerance and respect - indeed high appreciation - for every other. Minorities need protection and support, whether they be racial, ethnic, or religious.

2. Commitment to a culture of solidarity and a just economic order

Numberless men and women of all regions and religions strive to live their lives in solidarity with one another and to work for authentic fulfilment of their vocations. Nevertheless, all over the word we find endless hunger, deficiency, and need. Not only individuals, but especially unjust institutions and structures are responsible for these tragedies. Millions of people are without work; millions are exploited by poor wages, forced to the edges of society, with their possibilities for the future destroyed. In many lands the gap between the poor and the rich, between the powerful and the powerless is immense. We live in a world in which totalitarian state socialism as well as unbridled capitalism have hollowed out and destroyed many ethical and spiritual values. A materialistic mentality breeds greed for unlimited profit and a grasping for endless plunder. These demands claim more and more of the community's resources without obliging the individual to contribute more. The cancerous social evil of corruption thrives in the developing countries and in the developed countries alike.

(a) In the great ancient religious and ethical traditions of humankind we find the directive: **You shall not steal!** Or in positive terms: **Deal honestly and fairly!** Let us reflect anew on the consequences of this ancient directive: No one has the right to rob or dispossess in any way whatsoever any other person or the commonweal. Further, no one has the right to use her or his possessions without concern for the needs of society and Earth.

(b) Where extreme poverty reigns, helplessness and despair spread, and theft occurs again and again for the sake of survival. Where power and wealth are accumulated ruthlessly, feelings of envy, resentment, and deadly hatred and rebellion inevitably well up in the disdavantaged and marginalized. This leads to a vicious circle of

27

violence and counter-violence. Let no one be deceived: There is no global peace without global justice!

(c) Young people must learn at home and in school that property, limited though it may be, carries with it an obligation, and that its uses should at the same time serve the common good. Only thus can a **just economic order** be built up.

(d) If the plight of the poorest billions of humans on this planet, particularly women and children, is to be improved, the world economy must be structured more justly. Individual good deeds, and assistance projects, indispensable though they be, are insufficient. The participation of all states and the authority of international organizations are needed to build just economic institutions.

A solution which can be supported by all sides must be sought for the debt crisis and the poverty of the dissolving Second World, and even more the Third World. Of course conflicts of interest are unavoidable. In the developed countries, a distinction must be made between necessary and limitless consumption, between socially beneficial and non-beneficial uses of property, between justified and unjustified uses of natural resources, and between a profit-only and a socially beneficial and ecologically oriented market economy. Even the developing nations must search their national consciences.

Wherever those ruling threaten to repress those ruled, wherever institutions threaten persons, and wherever might oppresses right, we have an obligation to resist - whenever possible non-violently.

(e) To be authentically human in the spirit of our great religious and ethical traditions means the following:

We must utilize economic and political power for **service to humanity** instead of misusing it in ruthless battles for domination. We must develop a spirit of compassion with those who suffer, with special care for the children, the aged, the poor, the disabled, the refugees, and the lonely.

We must cultivate **mutual respect** and consideration, so as to reach a reasonable balance of interests, instead of thinking only of unlimited power and unavoidable competitive struggles.

We must value **a sense of moderation and modesty** instead of an unquenchable greed for money, prestige, and consumption! In greed humans lose their 'souls', their freedom, their composure, their inner peace, and thus that which makes them human.

3. Commitment to a culture of tolerance and a life of truthfulness

Numberless women and men of all regions and religions strive to lead lives of honesty and truthfulness. Nevertheless, all over the world we find endless lies and deceit, swindling and hypocrisy, ideology and demagoguery:

- Politicians and business people who use lies as a means to success;
- Mass media which spread ideological propaganda instead of accurate reporting, misinformation

instead of information, cynical commercial interest instead of loyalty to the truth;

- Scientists and researchers who give themselves over to morally questionable ideological or political programmes or to economic interest groups, or who justify research which violates fundamental ethical values;

- Representatives of religions who dismiss other religions as of little value and who preach fanaticism and intolerance instead of respect and understanding.

(a) In the great ancient religious and ethical traditions of humankind we find the directive: **You shall not lie!** Or in positive terms: **Speak and act truthfully!** Let us reflect anew on the consequences of this ancient directive: No woman or man, no institution, no state or church or religious community has the right to speak lies to other humans.

(b) This is especially true:

- For those who work in the **mass media**, to whom we entrust the freedom to report for the sake of truth and to whom we thus grant the office of guardian. They do not stand above morality but have the obligation to respect human dignity, human rights, and fundamental values. They are duty-bound to objectivity, fairness, and the preservation of human dignity. They have no right to intrude into individuals' private spheres, to manipulate public opinion, or to distort reality.

- For **artists, writers, and scientists,** to whom we entrust artistic and academic freedom. They are not exempt from general ethical standards and must serve the truth;

- For the **leaders of countries, politicians, and political parties,** to whom we entrust our own freedoms. When they lie in the faces of their people, when they manipulate the truth, or when they are guilty of venality or ruthlessnes in domestic or foreign affairs, they forsake their credibility and deserve to lose their offices and their voters. Conversely, public opinion should support those politicians who dare to speak the truth to the people at all times.

- Finally, for **representatives of religion.** When they stir up prejudice, hatred, and enmity towards those of different belief, or even incite or legitimate religious wars, they deserve the condemnation of humankind and the loss of their adherents.

Let no one be deceived, There is no global justice without truthfulness and humaneness!

(c) Young people must learn at home and in school to think, speak, and act **truthfully.** They have a right to information and education to be able to make the decisions that will form their lives. Without an ethical formation they will hardly be able to distinguish the important from the unimportant. In the daily flood of information, ethical standards will help them discern when opinions are portrayed as facts, interests veiled, tendencies exaggerated, and facts twisted.

(d) To be authentically human in the spirit of our great religious and ethical traditions means the following:

- We must not confuse freedom with arbitrariness or pluralism with indifference to truth.

- We must cultivate **truthfulness** in all our relationships instead of dishonesty, dissembling, and opportunism.

- We must **constantly seek truth** and incorruptible sincerity instead of spreading ideological or partisan half-truths.

- We must courageously **serve the truth** and we must remain **constant and trustworthy**, instead of yielding to opportunistic accommodation to life.

4. Commitment to a culture of equal rights and partnership between men and women

Numberless men and women of all regions and religions strive to live their lives in a spirit of partnership and responsible action in the areas of love, sexuality, and family. Nevertheless all over the world there are condemnable forms of patriarchy, domination of one sex over the other, exploitation of women, sexual misuse of children, and forced prostitution. Too frequently, social inequities force women and even children into prostitution as a means of survival - particularly in less developed countries.

(a) In the great ancient religious and ethical traditions of humankind we find the directive: **You shall not commit sexual immorality!** Or in positive terms: **Respect and love one another!** Let us reflect anew on the consequences of this ancient directive: No one has the right to degrade others to mere sex objects, to lead them into or hold them in sexual dependency.

(b) We condemn sexual exploitation and sexual discrimination as one of the worst forms of human degradation. We have the duty to resist wherever the domination of one sex over the other is preached - even in the name of religious conviction; wherever sexual exploitation is tolerated, wherever prostitution is fostered or children are misused. Let no one be deceived: There is no authentic humaneness without a living together in partnership!

(c) Young people must learn at home and in school that sexuality is not a negative, destructive, or exploitative force, but creative and affirmative. Sexuality as a life-affirming shaper of community can only be effective when partners accept the responsibilities of caring for one another's happiness.

(d) The relationship betwen women and men should be characterized not by patronizing behaviour or exploitation, but by love, partnership, and trustworthiness. Human fulfilment is not identical with sexual pleasure. Sexuality should express and reinforce a loving relationship lived by equal partners.

Some religious traditions know the ideal of a voluntary renunciation of the full use of sexuality. Voluntary renunciation also can be an expression of identity and meaningful fulfilment.

(e) The social institution of marriage, despite all its cultural and religious variety, is characterized by love, loyalty, and permanence. It aims at and should guarantee security and mutual support to husband, wife, and child. It should secure the rights of all family members. All lands and cultures should develop economic and social relationships which will enable marriage and family life worthy of human beings, especially for older people. Children have a right of access to education. Parents should not exploit children, nor children parents. Their relationships should reflect mutual respect, appreciation, and concern.

(f) To be authentically human in the spirit of our great religious and ethical traditions means the following:

We need mutual respect, **partnership**, and understanding, instead of patriarchal domination and degradation, which are expressions of violence and engender counter-violence.

We need mutual concern, tolerance, readiness for reconciliation, and **love**, instead of any form of possessive lust or sexual misuse.

Only what has already been experienced in personal and familial relationships can be practised on the level of nations and religions.

IV. A transformation of consciousness

Historical experience demonstrates the following: Earth cannot be changed for the better unless we achieve a transformation in the consciousness of individuals and in public life. The possibilities for transformation have already been glimpsed in areas such as war and peace, economy, and ecology, where in recent decades fundamental changes have taken place. This transformation must also be achieved in the area of ethics and values! Every individual has intrinsic dignity and inalienable rights, and each also has an inescapable responsibility for what she or he does and does not do. All our decisions and deeds, even our omissions and failures, have consequences.

Keeping this sense of responsibility alive, deepening it and passing it on to future generations, is the special task of religions. We are realistic about what we have achieved in this consensus, and so we urge that the following be observed.

1. A universal consensus on **many disputed ethical questions** (from bio- and sexual ethics through mass media and scientific ethics to economic and political ethics) will be difficult to attain. Nevertheless, even for many controversial questions, suitable solutions should be attainable in the spirit of the fundamental principles we have jointly developed here.

2. In many areas of life a new consciousness of ethical responsibility has already arisen. Therefore we would be pleased if as many **professions** as possible, such as those of physicians, scientists, business people, journalists, and politicians would develop up-to-date **codes of ethics** which would provide specific guidelines for the vexing questions of these particular professions.

3. Above all, we urge the various **communities of faith** to formulate their very **specific ethic**: what does each

faith tradition have to say, for example, about the meaning of life and death, the enduring of suffering and the forgiveness of guilt, about selfless sacrifice and the necessity of renunciation, about compassion and joy? These will deepen, and make more specific, the already discernible global ethic.

In conclusion, we appeal to all the inhabitants of this planet. Earth cannot be changed for the better unless the consciousness of individuals is changed. We pledge to work for such transformation in individual and collective consciousness, for the awakening of our spiritual powers through reflection, meditation, prayer, or positive thinking, for a **conversion of the heart**. Together we can move mountains! Without a willingness to take risks and a readiness to sacrifice there can be no fundamental change in our situation! Therefore we commit ourselves to a common global ethic, to better mutual under-standing, as well as to socially-beneficial, peace-fostering, and Earth-friendly ways of life.

We invite all men and women, whether religious or not, to do the same.

This was subscribed to by:

Bahai

Juana Conrad - Jacqueline Delahunt - Dr Wilma Ellis - Charles Nolley - R. Leilani Smith - Yael Wurmfeld.

Brahma Kumaris

B.K. Jagdish Chander Hassija - B.K. Dadi Prakashmani.

Buddhism

Rev. Koshin Ogui, Sensei. **Mahayana:** Rev. Chung Ok Lee. **Theravada:** Dr A.T. Ariyaratne - Preah Maha Ghosananda - Ajahn Phra Maha Surasak Jîvanando - Dr Chatsumarn Kabilsingh - Luang Poh Panyananda - Ven. Achahn Dr Chuen Phangcham Ven. Dr Havanpola Ratanasara - Ven. Dr Mapalagama Wipulasara Maha Thero. **Vajrayana:** His Highness the Fourteenth Dalai Lama. **Zen:** Prof. Masao Abe - Zen Master Seung Sahn - Rev. Samu Sunim.

Christianity

Blouke Carus - Dr Yvonne Delk. **Anglican:** Rev. Marcus Braybrooke - James Parks Morton. **Orthodox** Maria Svolos Gebhard. **Protestant** Dr Thelma Adair - Martti Ahtisaari - Rev. Wesley Ariarajah - Dr Gerald O. Barney - Dr Nelvia M. Brady - Dr David Breed - Rev. John Buchanan - Bishop R. Sheldon Duecker - Prof. Diana L. Eck - Dr Leon D. Finney, Jr - Dr James A. Forbes, Jr - Bishop Frederick C. James - Archbishop Mikko Juva - Prof. James Nelson - Dr David Ramage, Jr - Robert Reneker - Rev. Dr Syngman Rhee - Rev. Margaret Orr Thomas - Prof. Carl Friedrich von Weizsäcker - Prof. Henry Wilson - Rev. Addie Wyatt. **Roman Catholic** Rev. Thomas A. Baima - Cardinal Joseph Bernardin - Fr Pierre-François de Béthune - Sister Joan M. Chatfield MM - Rev. Theodore M. Hesburgh CSC - Abbot Timothy Kelly OSB - Jim Kenney - Prof. Hans Küng - Dolores Leakey - Sister Joan Monica McGuire OP - Rev. Maximilian Mizzi - Dr Robert Muller - Rev. Albert Nambiaparambil - Bishop

Placido Rodriguez - Bishop Willy Romélius - Dorothy Savage - Brother David Steindl-Rast OSB - Brother Wayne Teasdale.

Native religions

His Imperishable Glory Bambi Baaba. Akuapi: Nana Apeadu. Yoruba: His Royal Highness Oseijeman Adefunmi I - Baba Metahochi Kofi Zannu. Native American: Archie Mosay - Burton Pretty On Top - Peter V. Catches.

Hinduism

Dr M. Aram - Jayashree Athavale-Talwarkar - His Highness Swami Chidananda Saraswati - Swami Chidananda Saraswati Muniji - Swami Dayananda Saraswati - Sadguru Sant Keshavadas - P.V. Krishnayya - Dr Lakshmi Kumari- Amrish Mahajan - Dr Krishna Reddy - Prof. V. Madhusudan Reddy - Swami Satchidananda - His Highness Satguru Sivaya Subramuniyaswami - His Highness Dr Bala Siva Yogindra Maharaj. Vedanta: Pravrajika Amalaprana - Pravrajika Prabuddhaprana - Pravrajika Vivekaprana.

Jainism

Dr Rashmikant Gardi. Digambar: Narendra P. Jain. Shwetambar: His Highness Shri Atmanandji - Dipchand S. Gardi - His Excellence Dr L.M. Singhvi - His Highness Acharya Sushil Kumarji Maharaj.

Judaism

Helen Spector - Sir Sigmund Sternberg. Conservative: Professor Susannah Heschel. Reform: Rabbi Herbert Bronstein - Norma U. Levitt - Rabbi A. James Rudin - Rabbi Herman Schaalman - Dr Howard A. Sulkin. Orthodox: Prof. Ephraim Isaac.

Islam

Tan Sri Dato' Seri Ahmad Sarji bin Abdul-Hamid - Dr Qazi Ashfaq Ahmed - Hamid Ahmed - Mazar Ahmed - Hon. Louis Farrakhan - Dr Hamid Abdul Hai - Mohammed A. Hai - Dr Mohammad Hamidullah - Dr Aziza al-Hibri - Dr Asad Husain

- Dato Dr Haji Ismail bin Ibrahim - Dr Irfan Ahmat Khan - Qadir H. Khan - Dr Abdel Rahman Osman. Shi'ite: Prof. Seyyed Hossein Nasr. **Sunni:** Imam Dawud Assad - Imam Warith Deen Mohammed - Hon. Syed Shahabuddin.

Neo-pagans

Rev. Baroness Cara-Marguerite-Drusilla - Rev. Deborah Ann Light - Lady Olivia Robertson.

Sikhs

Siri Singh Sahbi Bhai Sahib Harabhajan Singh Khalsa Yogiji - Bhai Mohinder Singh - Dr Mehervan Singh - Hardial Singh - Indarjit Singh - Singh Sahib Jathedar Manjit Singh - Dr Balwant Singh Hansra.

Taoists

Chungliang Al Huang.

Theosophists

Radha Burnier.

Zoroastrians

Dastoor Dr Kersey Antia - Dr Homi Dhalla - Dastoor Dr Kaikhusroo Minocher JamaspAsa - - Dastoor Jehangir Oshidari - Rohinton Rivetna - Homi Taleyarkhan - Dastoor Kobad Zarolit- Dastoor Mehraban Zarthosty.

Inter-religious organizations

Karl Berzolheimer - Dr Daniel Gómez-Ibáñez - Ma Jaya Bhagavati - Peter Laurence - Dr Karan Singh - John B. Taylor - Rev. Robert Traer - Dr William F. Vendley.

In addition there were a number of signatures which could no longer be identified.

Commentaries and Background

The History, Significance and Method of the Declaration Toward a Global Ethic

Hans Küng

It was a historic week, the week from 28 August to 4 September 1993, during which the delegates of the Parliament of the World's Religions discussed the Declaration Toward a Global Ethic and then - the vast majority of them - signed it. The beginning of that week had brought the sensational news that Israel and the Palestine Liberation Organization (PLO) had agreed on a peace plan. In concrete terms that meant mutual recognition by the two arch-enemies and limited autonomy for parts of the occupied Palestinian territories. All at once prospects for a lasting peace in the Middle East had increased considerably. But this was a peace towards which the religions and their representatives - the representatives of Judaism, Islam and Christianity - should have made a greater contribution than they had done previously, by each opposing the fundamentalists in its own ranks. For there can be no peace among the nations without peace among the religions!

However, in that same week the peace negotiations between the Orthodox Serbs, the Catholic Croats and the Muslim Bosnians had collapsed again. And there is no doubt that the religions which are also involved here had neglected in the period of more than forty years since the Second World War to engage in mourning, honestly confess the crimes which had been committed by all sides in the course of the centuries, and ask one another for mutual forgiveness. Similarly, there is no doubt that the Catholic and Orthodox churches in particular have identified themselves all too much with their own political leadership in the most recent controversies and not made a commitment for peace openly, opportunely and energetically. Again I think that there can be no peace among the nations without peace among the religions!

Still, I found it significant that the Finnish negotiator in Geneva for peace in Bosnia-Herzegovina, the diplomat Martti Ahtisaari, as I was told, had in his hands not only the draft plan for peace in this region but also the Declaration of the Parliament of the World's Religions Toward a Global Ethic and signed it immediately as the right word at the right time. And I have no doubt that the President of the International Committee of the Red Cross in Geneva, Dr Cornelio Sommaruga, would also have put his personal signature to this declaration, which incorporates so many principles of the International Red Cross, had he not been prevented in principle from signing any such declarations because of the need for his high office to be neutral. For there can be no human survival without a common human ethic, a global ethic!

The Red Cross, which grew out of a small 'Committee' around Henri Dumant and is therefore still called the 'Committee of the Red Cross' today, is perhaps the most hopeful example of how quite a small group can stand at the origins of a great initiative which initially does not seem very hopeful, yet in the end can have world-wide influence. The Declaration Toward a Global Ethic also goes back to the bold initiative of a very small group: I want to tell its story briefly here.

1. The prehistory

Since 1989 I had been in contact with the local group which was interested in a centenary celebration of the First Parliament of World Religions in Chicago in September 1993. Karl-Joseph Kuschel will describe in the next chapter what this first World Parliament was and how the second World Parliament differed from it.

From 7 to 10 February 1989 a colloquium had taken place at UNESCO in Paris for which I wrote the basic paper; I was also able to suggest the names of people to respond to it. It was entitled 'Pas de paix entre les nations sans paix entre les religions', and the respondents, all professors, were Masao Abe (Kyoto) for Buddhism, Mohammed Arkoun (Paris) for Islam, Eugene B. Borowitz (New York) for Judaism, Claude Geffré (Paris) for Christianity, Liu Shu-hsien (Hong Kong) for Chinese religion, Bithika Mukerji (Benares) for Hinduism and Karl Josef Partsch (Bonn) from the perspective of international law.

On 9-10 March 1989 I gave similar lectures at the universities of Toronto and Chicago: 'No peace among the nations without peace among the religions'. In the lecture in the Rockefeller Chapel of the University of Chicago I called on those responsible for planning the centenary celebration of the 1893 World Parliament of Religions to proclaim a century later a 'new ethical consensus' of the religions. However, it was all still very unclear at that time, apart from two things. First, the second Parliament should not be left to a certain religious sect with considerable financial resources which had already shown interest in it. And secondly, the Divinity School of the University of Chicago - where I had been visiting professor in the winter semester of 1981 and had had rich scholarly inter-religious experiences - did not want to involve itself in the matter as such. However, on my return to Tübingen I received an invitation dated 28 April 1989 from the then Administrator of the Council for a Parliament of the World's Religions, Ron Kidd, with whom I had spoken, to draft the first outline of a declaration on a common ethic for the Parliament in collaboration with a team in Chicago. I agreed in principle, but the plans for the trip to Chicago that was needed and a planned meeting in Washington on the occasion of a later lecture did not work out.[1]

My book *Global Responsibility* appeared in German in 1990. All my experiences with the problems of a global ethic, above all at UNESCO and also at the World Economic Forum in Davos, had come together in this book, and in it I could already discuss in breadth the need for a global ethic in the context of the world religions and the world economy. The next year an English-American edition had also appeared under the title *Global Responsibility. In Search of a New World Ethic.* The preface to this edition had been written by Prince Philip, Duke of Edinburgh - to whom I remain most deeply grateful - who remarked that in this book there was a discussion of 'what is probably the most critical and challenging issue in the debate about the future of the human habitation of this globe'.

1. Together with the Protestant theologian Jürgen Moltmann I was preparing a volume of the international theological journal *Concilium* for April 1990 devoted to the topic *The Ethics of World Religions and Human Rights*, which was meant to help to clarify the theoretical theme.

A pragmatic American, Professor Swidler of the Religion Department of Temple University, Philadelphia, and editor of the *Journal of Ecumenical Studies*, then composed an appeal in which among other things he called for the prompt composition of a declaration on a global ethic. Having become somewhat sceptical after my experiences with numerous actions and appeals of this kind, I personally responded at first in a somewhat restrained way, but in the end decided to become the first signatory to Swidler's appeal, after making some corrections. I also sought out some signatories in Europe. The key sentences from this declaration run: 'Such efforts should concentrate on drawing together the research and reflection on Global Ethic and related matters into a "Universal Declaration on a Global Ethos" which would then be circulated to the various forums of all the religions and ethical groups for appropriate revisions - with a view to eventual adoption by all the religions and ethical groups of the world. Such a "Universal Declaration of a World Ethic" could then serve a function similar to the 1948 "Universal Declaration of Human Rights" of the United Nations - a kind of standard that all will be expected to live up to ... The "Universal Declaration of Global Ethos" would in a major way bring to bear the moral and spiritual resources of all the religions and ethical groups on the basic ethical problems of the world, which are not easily susceptible to political force.'

So this appeal was finally published and was signed by important theologians and scholars in religious studies.[2] I myself had the opportunity to present the

2. Muhammed Arkoun (Muslim), Julia Ching (Confucian/Catholic), John Cobb (Methodist), Khalid Duran (Muslim), Heinrich Fries (Catholic), Claude Geffré (Catholic), Irving Greenberg (Jewish), Norbert Greinacher (Catholic), Riffat Hassan (Muslim), Rivka

declaration in connection with a further lecture to the UNESCO authorities in Paris and to discuss it with representatives of both Judaism and Islam, Rabbi René Samuel Sirat, President of the Permanent Council of the Conference of European Rabbis, and Tadjini Haddam, Rector of the Muslim Institute of the Great Mosque of Paris.

In the meantime of course *Global Responsibility* had also been read in Chicago, and on 27 February 1992 the 'Council' for the preparation of the World Parliament finally sent its Executive Director, Dr Daniel Gómez-Ibáñez, to Tübingen. His task was to persuade me definitively to undertake the draft of a Declaration by the Parliament on a Global Ethic, which I was to write in Tübingen. People in Chicago envisaged a document of two to three pages. However, it was clear to me that things could not be done this way if the aim was to provide more than a casual 'poster'. Of course a well-argued declaration could not be written in a few days or weeks. So when despite other burdens I finally promised to write a 'Declaration' for a 'Global Ethic' (not vaguely for 'Global Values', which was originally proposed by Chicago), I did so in awareness of the fact that the Parliament of the World's Religions provided a quite

Horwitz (Jewish), John Hick (Presbyterian), Gerfried Hunold (Catholic), Adel Khoury (Catholic), Paul Knitter (Catholic), Karl-Joseph Kuschel (Catholic), Pinchas Lapide (Jewish), Johannes Lähnemann (Protestant), Dietmar Mieth (Catholic), Paul Mojzes (Methodist), Jürgen Moltmann (Protestant), Fathi Osman (Muslim), Raimon Panikkar (Hindu/Buddhist/Catholic), Daniel Polish (Jewish), Rodolfo Stavenhagen (sociologist), Theo Sundermeier (Protestant), Tu Wei-Ming (Confucian). Cf. *Journal of Ecumenical Studies* 28.1, editorial, and *Süddeutsche Zeitung*, 16/17 November 1991.

unique opportunity for the concern for a global ethic. It was important to seize it.

2. The preparations for the text

I now devoted my teaching programme for the summer semester of 1992 completely to this theme. Instead of having a seminar on postmodernity, I held an inter-disciplinary and inter-religious *colloquium* on 'Human Rights - World Religions - World Ethic'. This time, too, I was able to rely on the friendship of Tübingen colleagues, the Indologist Heinrich von Stietencron and the Islamist Josef van Ess, with whom I had already given dialogue lectures on *Christianity and the World Religions* (which were published in 1984). Along with the Sinologist Professor Karl-Heinz Pohl they helped me to find competent dialogue partners from the other religions for this colloquium. At the same time they made a substantial contribution towards clarifying the funda-mental questions of principle by their own scholarly contributions.

During our colloquium the responses by distingu-ished representatives of the other religions were important for me: the contribution by the Chinese professor Li Zehou, living in exile, and the leading Thai Buddhist and social reformer Sulak Sivaraska, along with those of Rabbi Dr David Krochmalnik, the Hindu Dr Vasudha Dalmia, the Muslim Dr Roswitha Badry, and the Austrian Buddhist Alois Payer. Furthermore Dr Heiner Bielefeldt, an expert on human rights questions, helped us to examine the ethical potential of the 1948 United Nations Declaration of Human Rights and the 1949 Basic Law of the Federal Republic of Germany and to provide precise criteria for distinguishing between law and ethic, rights and ethics.

Nevertheless, at the end of the summer semester of 1992 I continued to be unclear how such a declaration should be structured and put into words. And everything depended on structure and style. The structure had to be clear (not over-complex) and the style totally comprehensible (no technical language). What should be the guidelines for such a declaration? The classical virtues? From the start that seemed to me rather boring. Or particular problem areas, which was the special wish of my students from our institute, who with the utmost commitment represented the younger generations? But this seemed to me to be simply too difficult in view of the complex problem areas of sexual and marital morality, the ethics of the economy, the media and the state.

As a first stage I had simply drafted a *preamble* and not only given it to our colloquium but at the beginning of June 1992 also sent it to several competent scholars in different world religions. I had built up my own *small consultative network*, which comprised correspondents from Europe to America, from Central Africa to Bangladesh. I also canvassed the idea at lectures throughout the world - those at the World Conference of Religions for Peace in Mainz, the World Congress of Faiths in London, the International Association for Religious Freedom in Hamburg, the Shalom Hartman Institute in Jerusalem, the World Economic Forum in Davos, the Temple of Understanding and the United Nations in New York were particularly important - and had countless discussions with believers of very different religions (and of course also with 'non-believers'). In particular I am most grateful for suggestions from the former Deputy General Secretary of the United Nations and Chancellor of the UNO Peace University in Costa Rica, Dr Robert Muller; the physicist and philosopher Carl-Friedrich von Weizsäcker of Starnberg; and the educational specialist Professor Reijo E. Heinonen of Turku, Finland, along with reactions from scholars in religion like Professor Julia Ching of Toronto, Professor Ursula King of Bristol and Professor Peter Antes of Hanover, not to forget Professor Johannes Lähnemann of Erlangen, an expert in religious education, who is organizing a Congress on 'Global Ethic and Education' in Nuremberg for autumn 1994.

On 14 July 1992 the *first draft* of the Universal Declaration was ready and was immediately sent to the experts for comments and corrections. Without exception it met with great approval; its basic structure remained unchanged, but it was considerably improved by numerous detailed suggestions. On 12 October 1992 the *second improved draft* was ready and on 23 October 1992, to my great relief, I could send the English translation prepared by Professor Leonard Swidler to Chicago in the hope that I would have corrections from there by the beginning of 1993, so that I could produce the definitive text.

However, there was now an unexpectedly long pause. My draft was discussed in the 'Council' in Chicago and made available to all the members of the Board of Trustees. Further experts were brought in and the discussion circle was extended.[3] Finally, various cardinals and bishops attentively studied the draft, as did scholars and monks of non-Christian religions. It was only on 13 June 1993

3. The main participants in the discussions in Chicago were Jeffrey Carlson (De Paul University), Manford Vogel (North-Western University), Robert Marshall (Lutheran School of Theology at Chicago = LSTC), Yoshiro Ishida (LSTC), Ilona Klemens (LSTC)

(in the middle of a summer semester now burdened with quite a different set of problems) that I finally received an answer from Dr Daniel Gómez-Ibáñez to the draft which I had sent in October 1992. But it was pleasantly positive: it called for improvements to the English translation and contained various suggestions for corrections to content and style, and also the short form of the Declaration that was desired.

Supported as always by my colleague Dr Karl-Josef Kuschel, who was to accompany me to the Parliament of the World's Religions, as best I could I incorporated all the corrections (along with others which had arrived in the meantime) and thus on 17 July 1993 - after further translation by Professor Swidler - was thus able to send the *definitive English text* to Chicago. There it underwent only further minor corrections and was approved by the Board of Trustees. The initial basic structure and language had remained the same through all the phases, but details of the text had been considerably improved. More than a hundred people from all the great religions had been involved in the process of consultation.

Unfortunately, however, it was now no longer possible, as had originally been planned, to present the

James A. Scherer (LSTC), Ron Kidd (Institute for World Spirituality), David Breed (CPWR), Kyaw Than (LSTC), Tanveer Azmat (Islamic Research Foundation), Infan Ahmad Khan (American Islamic College), John Kaserow (Catholic Theological Union), William Schweiker (University of Chicago, Divinity School), Charles Strain (De Paul University), Mary R. Garrison (De Paul University). Also consulted were Professor David Tracy (University of Chicago, Divinity School), Professor Robert Schreiter (Catholic Theological Union), Rabbi Herman Schaalman, Dr Ghulam Haider Aasi, Dr Chuen Phangcham, Dr Richard Luecke, the Ecumenical Officer of the Archdiocese of Chicago Thomas Baima, along with many others.

Declaration to some internationally known representatives of the great religions for examination and acceptance. The prior endorsement of religious and spiritual personalities would doubtless have eased the acceptance of the Declaration in the Parliament of the World's Religions and in public. Nor was the text of the Declaration immediately sent to all the members of the Parliament, as had previously been agreed, but only to the roughly 200 'delegates' of the various religions, and finally also - with an embargo which was soon broken - to the press. Finally, the text was discussed in the assembly of the delegates. I shall report on that in due course.

First, though, let us turn to the questions of hermeneutics and method which had to be considered in connection with a declaration on a global ethic.

3. What had to be avoided in a declaration on a global ethic

I readily acknowledge that for a long time I was quite perplexed as to what the content and style of such a declaration should be. On the one hand there were no historical models: for the first time in the history of the religions a declaration on an ethic was to be worked out which was to be acceptable to the adherents of all religions. But on the other hand for a long time I did not have the necessary intuition of the declaration as a whole, the perspective from which it should be written and the kind of language it should use. For the declaration that was envisaged had to be all of a piece, with no dry paragraph work, no colourful bouquet of quotations, no academic discourse, no diplomatic communiqué, none of those compromise products which usually emerge from committee work. 'The world has never been redeemed by a committee', John Courtney Murray once remarked to me during the Second Vatican Council. He was a pioneer American Catholic in a new democratic understanding of church and state, and author of the draft of the famous Declaration of the Second Vatican Council on Religious Liberty. Since then this sentence has been stamped on my mind. It was clear to me that though a declaration on a global ethic of course could not do without the 'input' of a great many heads, it needed a concept and a programme for developing the material.

In fact even the many inter-disciplinary discussions which I have reported, with their countless suggestions on points of detail, could not simply 'produce' an overall conception. But as a result of them, in succession I gained three essential insights.

1. It was indispensable - against the background of today's world - to make a clear distinction between the ethical level and the purely legal or political level and at the same time to give a precise definition of the term 'global ethic' (Part I).
2. The fundamental ethical demand on all men and women and all human societies or institutions should be a basic principle the beginnings of which one finds in every great religious or ethical tradition: 'Every human being must be treated humanely.' There was also the 'Golden Rule', which can similarly be demonstrated in all the great traditions: 'Do not do to another what you would not want to be done to you!' (Part II[4]).

4. I had long reflected on the fundamental ethical demand for truly human behaviour. Cf. H.Küng, *On Being a Christian* (1974), London and New York 1976, D II.1, 'Norms of the Human'; id.,

3. These fundamental ethical demands can be made concrete in four ancient directives which can also be found in all the great religions: 'Do not kill, do not steal, do not lie, do not commit sexual immorality' (Part III[5]).

In a friendly private meeting after the penultimate session of the colloquium on 2 July 1992, with my colleagues Li Zehou, Sulak Sivaraksa, Heinrich von Stietencron and Karl Heinz Pohl, it dawned on me what should be done about the third and most different concrete part, and that it could be shaped by those four ancient directives. But of course that had not yet answered the question how all this was to be done. There were various negative and positive criteria to be noted which had come home to me in the course of discussion.

First of all, negatively: what was the declaration on a global ethic *not* to be? To put it schematically:

(a) *No reduplication of the Declaration on Human Rights.* If religions essentially only repeated statements from the UN Declaration on Human Rights, one could do without such a declaration; however, an ethic is more than rights. And certainly such a declaration on an ethic would not escape the charge made especially by the Indian religions, that this was a typically 'Western' document.

Does God Exist? An Answer for Today (1978), London and New York 1980, Chapters E II 3, 'Fundamental Trust as the Basis for Ethics'; F IV4, 'Consequences for Ethics: Theologically Justified Autonomy'. This book also shows that this approach has little to do with the 'natural theology' which is feared above all by Protestant theologians of the Barthian school.
5. Here I could take up the beginnings of my *Global Responsibility* (Chapter A V1, 'Ethical Perspectives of the World Religions').

However, a declaration on a global ethic should provide ethical support for the UN Declaration on Human Rights, which is so often ignored, violated and evaded. Treaties, laws, agreements are observed only if there is an underlying ethical will really to observe them.

(b) *No political declaration*: if religions made concrete statements on questions which were directly related to world politics or economics like the Middle East conflict or the resolution of the debt crisis, the difference between the political and the ethical levels would not be observed and the declaration on a global ethic would immediately be drawn into the maelstrom of world-political discussions and confrontations; it would deepen the political dissent rather than bridge it. So no specific modern Western theory of the state or society can form the basis of such a declaration.

However, a declaration on a global ethic should also have relevance at the economic and political levels and support efforts towards a just ordering of the economy and of society.

(c) *No casuistic moral sermon.* If religions only admonished with a raised finger or a threatening fist; got lost in a flood of commandments and precepts, canons and paragraphs; indeed wanted to make binding statements on every possible difficult case (even in so popular an area as sexual ethics), they would be *a priori* rejected by many people today and certainly not be able to produce a consensus. To enter into moral questions like divorce or euthanasia which are disputed in all religions and nations would be to torpedo such a declaration from the start.

However, a declaration on a global ethic should not hesitate to make clear statements even about uncomfortable truths and demands - like respect for all life - and should not leave out the sexual sphere.

(d) *No philosophical treatise.* If religions relied on a modern philosophical ethics, whether inspired more by analytic linguistic philosophy, Frankfurt Critical Theory, or a theory of history, they would presumably hardly get beyond problematical generalizations and pragmatic models (with transcendental, utilitarian or even regional bases). However a declaration on a global ethic should address more than intellectuals or educated people.

Still, a declaration on a global ethic should readily take up all the stimuli provided by philosophy and should be formulated in such a way that philosophers - and indeed also agnostics and atheists - could accept it, even if they did not share the transcendent ground of such a declaration.

(e) *No enthusiastic religious proclamation.* If religions simply invoke cosmic consciousness, global harmony, spiritual creativity, universal unity, all-embracing love and a spiritual vision of a better world, or hymn mother earth and in so doing do not take sufficiently seriously the economic, political and social reality of today's highly complex industrial society, they are alienating themselves from reality, as far as both the world and they themselves are concerned. On the other hand a consensus of religions on a particular anthropology (e.g. the relationship of body and soul) or a particular metaphysics (e.g. the relationship of space, time and supreme being or self) is not to be expected and therefore is not to be expressed in a declaration on a global ethic.

However, a declaration of the religions on a global ethic should clearly indicate that it is a declaration by men and women with a religious motivation who are convinced that the present empirical world is not the ultimate, supreme, 'absolute' spiritual reality and truth.

4. What a declaration on a global ethic should contain

Along with these negative demarcations came some positive pointers, which I shall now list. In positive terms, what should a declaration on a global ethic contain? Programmatically, such a declaration
- must penetrate to a deeper *ethical level*, the level of *binding values, irrevocable criteria* and *inner basic attitudes*, and not remain stuck at the legal level of laws, codified rights and paragraphs with which issue might be taken, or at the political level of proposing concrete political solutions. Despite all its consequences for specific areas, an ethic is primarily concerned with the inner realm of a person, the sphere of the conscience, of the 'heart', which is not directly exposed to sanctions that can be imposed by political power (the power of the state, the courts, the police);
- must be capable of *securing a consensus:* moral unanimity and not just numerical unanimity is to be striven for. So statements should be avoided which are a priori rejected by one of the great religions. Condemnations which are understood as a violation of religious feelings are counter-productive;
- must be *self-critical:* the declaration should not just be addressed to the 'world', but also and primarily to the

religions themselves. Their frequent failure, particularly in making peace, should not be concealed, but be stated unequivocally. To this degree such a declaration must have the character not only of gentle confirmation but of constructive provocation;

- must be *related to reality*. From beginning to end the world must be seen as it really is and not just as it should be. So the starting point must always be what is, with a progression from there to what should be. To recognize the real significance of norms which initially seem general it is necessary to begin with certain negative experiences. What is truly human is not always easy to divine, but anyone can give a few examples of what is really inhuman;

- must be *generally comprehensible*: technical arguments and scientific jargon, of whatever origin, are to be avoided. Everything must be expressed in a language which at least the ordinary newspaper reader can understand and which can also be translated into other languages. It is not rationalism to avoid irrational statements; it is not irrationalism to remain open to the super-rational ('beyond the limits of pure reason');

- must have *a religious foundation*: even if all men and women are to be addressed, including those who are not religious, it should be made plain that for religions, an ethic has a religious foundation. For those with a religious motivation, an ethic has to do with trust (quite rational trust) in an ultimate supreme reality, whatever name this may be given and no matter what the dispute over its nature may be among the different religions.

The declaration should have the name 'Declaration Toward a Global Ethic', not 'Global Ethics'. 'Ethic' means a basic human moral attitude, whereas 'ethics' denotes the philosophical or theological theory of moral attitudes, values and norms. Unfortunately, it is not as easy to make this distinction in all languages as it is in German, as I already noted in connection with the translations of my book *Projekt Weltethos*, which in English became *Global Responsibility*. Thus the Greek word 'ethos' is not used much in most languages, and even the term 'world' cannot be combined with 'ethos' or 'ethic' in a word as it can be in German, where we talk quite naturally of world history, world politics, world economy, world society, using a single word. The result of the discussion with translators and publishers was that the following terms would be used for the German 'Weltethos':

- in English 'world ethic' or 'global ethic' (not 'ethics', which like the German word 'Ethik' means the doctrine or the system),
- in French 'éthique planétaire'
- in Spanish 'ética mundial'
- in Italian, 'etica mondiale',
- in Czech 'světový étos', and so on.

However, the choice of word is not ultimately decisive here. It is the subject-matter, not the name, which is important. Anyone who even in German prefers for whatever reason to speak of global, universal or planetary ethics can of course do so. These terms refer to the same thing. However, 'Weltethos' has already become established as 'global ethic'.

Still, particularly in view of the religious character of the declaration, from the beginning the difficult question now arises: should such a declaration be promulgated as it were in the name of God? To Christians, Jews and Muslims that seems a matter of course, but it is not.

5. In the name of God? The Buddhists' objection

If all religions were to be involved in a declaration on a global ethic and at least no important ones were to be excluded, then one would have to dispense with naming God: this was clear to me from the beginning, reluctant though I was to accept it as a Christian theologian. 'In the name of God, the almighty, creator of heaven and earth': certainly it would have been easier to argue in this way in respect of unconditionally valid norms. But in that case one would have to have left out *Buddhism*, one of the great world religions. It was clear to me from the start that the representatives of Buddhism would not have accepted the name of God in such a declaration. And moreover there was immediately a controversy over this even during the Parliament. So I want to explain this point in more detail.

Buddhism - a *religion without God?* Of course experts in Buddhism can point out that Buddhism as practised *in reality* does know 'God', indeed a number of gods taken over from popular religion (Indian religion or some others): those personified natural forces or divinized kings and saints who are called on for protection and help (there are phenomena corresponding to such practical polytheism in popular Catholicism with its veneration of saints and angels). The Buddha Gautama himself regarded the gods (*devas*) as real but provisional, since they too were subject to birth and rebirth.

On the other hand, for Buddhists divine beings have a form of of being far beyond human beings. So for the Buddha, who always regards himself as a human being and not a god, it is quite consistent to gain the help of the gods for this-worldly matters not related to redemption (rain, the blessing of children - just as in Christianity heavenly helpers, angels and archangels standing near to God are often invoked for help). In short, in Buddhism there are gods, and these are to be venerated, as numerous passages in the Pali canon commend. So in the sphere of Buddhism we do not find a strict atheism but a polytheism - often crudely magical. However, the gods are not 'Ultimate Reality', absolute 'Ground' and 'Primal Goal'. So there was need for caution in a common invocation of the name of God in a declaration on a global ethic.

For of course Christians, and with them Jews and Muslims - the three religions of a Semitic Near Eastern origin and prophetic character - do not mean by the name of God one god among many, not even the highest, but the one and only God, Creator and Perfecter of the world and human beings. And of course in this understanding, 'God' is the 'last and first reality'. But Buddhism sees God against an Indian horizon: he is like the Indian god Brahman who is proudly enthroned on the pyramid of gods and is similarly subject to coming to be and passing away. As for a personal creator God, Buddha Gautama already confessed his ignorance and his indifference: completely intent on redeeming human beings from suffering, he rejects answers to speculative questions like those about God and the origin of the world. In this sense, on this higher level, Buddhism is, if not atheistic, at least resolutely agnostic.

Now a rational *dialogue* about this basic difference, too, is quite *possible* between the monotheistic prophetic religions and the different branches of Buddhism (Theravada, Mahayana and Vajrayana). It is a dialogue which has to concentrate on the comparison of the concept of God with the basic Buddhist concepts of Nirvana, Shunyata and Dharmakaya. These are all terms which the great majority of Buddhists do not understand in a nihilistic way but as a positive reality, and which can be regarded by Christians as parallel terms for the Absolute. They fulfil analogous functions to the concept of God. At an earlier stage, when as a theologian I was naturally interested not only in the ethical but also and primarily in 'dogmatic questions' (of faith), I tried to describe how for a deeper Jewish-Christian-Muslim understanding of God (as the last/first, highest/deepest reality) God himself is all this in one:

- 'Nirvana', in so far as he is the goal of the way of redemption;
- 'Shunyata' (void), in so far as he continually escapes all affirmative definitions;
- 'Dharmakaya' (body of teaching), in so far as law governs the cosmos and human beings;
- 'Adi Buddha' (primal Buddha), in so far as he is the origin of all.[6]

But these brief remarks show clearly enough that here we come up against an extremely difficult problem, and that we did well to avoid naming the name of God in our Declaration Toward a Global Ethic. The reaction of Buddhists during the Parliament confirmed this. For because some religious leaders of the various guest committees, with the best intentions in the world, had quite ingenuously used the names 'God the Almighty' and 'God the Creator' in their invocations, prayers and blessings at the opening plenary and on other occasions,

6. For these difficult problems see H. Küng (with J. von Ess, H. von Stietencron and H. Bechert), *Christianity and the World Religions. An Introduction to Dialogue with Islam, Hinduism and Buddhism* (1984), New York and London 1986, Chapter C III 2: 'Buddhism - atheistic?'

and had spoken of the need to 'strive for a unity of religions under God', *leading Buddhists during the Parliament felt called on to protest.*

At the beginning of the first session of the 'Assembly' of the religious leaders, the Ven. Samu Sunim of the Zen Buddhist Temple in Chicago read out a statement[7] in which he complained of the lack of knowledge and sensitivity on the part of certain religious leaders: 'With great astonishment we watched leaders of different traditions define all religions as religions of God and unwittingly rank Buddha with God.' And because this had happened, the Buddhists now wanted to state: 'We would like to make it known to all that Shakyamuni (Gautama) Buddha, the founder of Buddhism, was not God or a god. He was a human being who attained full Enlightenment through meditation and showed us the path of spiritual awakening and freedom. Therefore, Buddhism is not a religion of God. Buddhism is a religion of wisdom, enlightenment and compassion. Like the worshippers of God who believe that salvation is available to all through confession of sin and a life of prayer, we Buddhists believe that salvation and enlightenment is available to all through removal of defilements and delusion and a life of meditation. However, unlike those who believe in God who is separate from us, Buddhists believe that Buddha which means "one who is awake and enlightened" is inherent in us all as Buddhanature or Buddhamind.'

7. The statement was also signed by the supreme patriarch of Cambodian Buddhism, Ven. Maha Ghosananda, by Zen Master Seung Sahn, by the Ven. Abbot Walpola Piyananda (Sri Lanka Buddhism), the Rev. Chung Ok Lee (Korean Buddhism) and the Thai professor Chatsumarn Kabilsingh.

However, this statement by the Buddhists was by no means limited to criticism. Apart from the invitation to take seriously the different approaches of the religions to spirituality and salvation as a prerequisite for a Parliament of the World's Religions, two of their concerns seem to me to be particularly welcome:

- The *affirmation of concern for a global ethic*: 'We feel that we the religious leaders of the world gathered here at this historic Parliament of the World's Religions must establish strong guidelines for religious tolerance and cooperation and serve as inspirations for the different religious communities in the world.'

- The *concern for language and communication:* 'We must train ourselves to be sensitive to each other and learn to use language which is inclusive and all-embracing. We suggest we use "Great Being" or "power of the transcendent" or "Higher Spiritual Authority" instead of God in reference to the ultimate spiritual reality. We are open to other suggestions and discussions on this matter.'

This abundantly confirms what I have already said myself about a deeper understanding of God in the light of the Buddhist tradition.

6. Disputed questions

The Buddhist objections to the use of the name of God, which were heard by the delegates in respectful silence, were already evidence that a consensus can be achieved in matters relating to a global ethic only if, as I suggested in my *Global Responsibility*, one leaves aside all differences of faith and 'dogma', symbols and rites, and concentrates on common guidelines for human conduct. That is true not only in connection with dogmatic demands by Christians but also in connection with the demands from the sphere of the Indian religions (which are often no less dogmatic), when these for example presuppose a universality of ideas (for example about consciousness and supreme being) which does not in fact exist, or even assert a unity of spiritual experience and thus of the religions. In so doing they sometimes neglect all the divisive differences among the religions, something which is only possible on the basis of a pantheistic or mystical view of unity (Brahman = Atman) which is not even capable of commanding a consensus.

Of course there were further discussions within the framework of the 'Assembly' of religious leaders. But these were to relate above all to the future of the Parliament of Religions and questions about collaboration. The Declaration itself had already gone through a process of wide inter-religious consultation and had been accepted. Given the complexity of the problems and the limitations of time it was hardly possible to hold an effective discussion, and so no discussion in the Parliament had originally been provided for (the 1990 Seoul Church Assembly had been a warning to us!). All that had been sought had been a free testimony to the assent of all participants (and not just the 'delegates') who wanted to sign - on the basis of their insight into the text, the consultation that had taken place, and the authority of the first internationally known signatories who had originally attached their names to the Declaration.

However, this was not what happened. Contrary to the original agreement, the 'Council' had held back the Declaration Toward a Global Ethic so as to be able to present it at the end as an effective conclusion - not least with the media in view. It had been supplied to the 'Assembly', but with the proviso that now they could only discuss it, and could not make any changes. But that led to objections (understandable in some, but not all respects) from those who rejected the procedure itself (which had not been explained at all to the delegates) and encouraged those who had problems with individual points of content. By far the majority of critics had no idea of the broad process of inter-religious consultation which had been connected with the composition of the Declaration.

Furthermore, because of the situation I have described, the 'Assembly' discussed not only the Declaration Toward a Global Ethic but also practical and political questions. In particular, representatives of the native Indian population of America and Black Americans used this assembly to propose verbal motions, presented on the spot, in support of their concerns (which are all too justified), without there being time to discuss these seriously. The lack of an agenda made it difficult for the Chairperson of the Assembly, Dr David Ramage, to bring order to a debate which often became passionate. Finally, in view of the various motions, he decided that the 'Assembly', which had no legislative competence, had to refrain from voting on any resolutions whatsoever.

As far as the Declaration Toward a Global Ethic was concerned, the proposal of a Muslim to demote it to a working paper did not secure a majority. Since the discussion of the Declaration took place at the first session of the 'Assembly' at separate round tables, it was not easy to discover where the objections lay. But three points seem to have played a part.

(a) In the section on the culture of *non-violence* some people - particularly in view of the desparate situation of the Muslims in Bosnia - felt that the *right to self-defence* (which is also affirmed by the United Nations Charter) was not brought out clearly enough. To that, of course, it can be replied that the Declaration deliberately took a middle course which could secure a consensus: between a 'Realpolitik' of force in resolving conflicts and an unrealistic unconditional pacifism which, confronted with violence, expulsion, rape, death and mass murder, unconditionally repudiates the use of force. First of all the Declaration states in principle: 'Such conflicts, however, should be resolved without violence within a framework of justice. This is true for states as well as for individuals.' However, it immediately adds: 'Persons who hold political power must work within the framework of a just order and commit themselves to the most non-violent, peaceful solutions possible. And they should work for this within an international order of peace which itself has need of protection and defence against perpetrators of violence' (III 1 b). And in connection with the legal and economic order it is stated: 'Wherever those ruling threaten to repress those ruled, wherever institutions threaten persons, and wherever might oppresses right, we are obligated to resist - whenever possible non-violently' (III 2 d).

It follows from this that the right to self-defence is clearly affirmed both for the individual and for the collective - but in the context of a culture of non-violence it applies only in extremis, in extreme instances, namely when non-violent resistance is senseless. In the face of brutality, barbarism and genocide, self-defence is said to be permissible. No further holocaust of any people whatever can simply be accepted in a pacifist way. On the other hand, no simple formula of legitimation for military intervention of any kind is to be offered: no 'just wars' in the service of interests which are all too clearly economic, political and military are to be justified in this way.

(b) Of course the objections to the culture of equal rights and the partnership of man and woman, made more in an underhand way than openly, also had to be taken seriously. It was claimed that the text of the Declaration said too little about the *family*; this could easily be refuted, given the statements about marriage, family and nurture, parents and children, but was provoked by the English translation which at some points had rendered the German 'in the family' with 'at home'.

However, it must be conceded that what is said in this section about *equal rights for women* doubtless presents a challenge not only to some Muslims and Hindus but also to more conservative European and American Christians. Certainly the Declaration deliberately says nothing about the role of women in worship; the ordination of women to the priesthood is a highly controversial question in most Christian churches and does not belong in any consensus document. But even without such a statement there are individual statements in this section about women which must prompt certain Christians, Muslims and Hindus to reflect on their own positions. It should be remembered that now we cannot just repeat ancient directives from our Holy Scriptures, including those relating to women, in a sterile way, but have to translate them into present-day terms. Not least as a result of Dostoievsky's perceptive legend of the Grand Inquisitor, Christians have become accustomed to asking: 'What would he (the Messiah Jesus) say if he were to come again?' Could not the analogous question be equally meaningful for Muslims: 'What would he (the Prophet Muhammad) say if he were to come again?'

Presumably both Jesus and Muhammad would have a good deal to say, particularly on the question of women.

(c) The objection had been expressed from one particular side that the whole Declaration was *'too Western'*. The objection did not go into detail, but the purport was probably that in this Declaration everything had not been reduced to keywords like 'cosmic consciousness', 'global spiritual harmony', 'bond with the universe', 'unity of soul and cosmos'. However, it must be conceded that of course a declaration will differ, depending on whether it has been drafted by a Thai monk, an Indian Swami, a Japanese Zen master, a Jewish Rabbi, a Muslim Ayatollah or a Christian theologian. Each has his own approach, his own style, and brings with it his own basic cultural and religious colouring. I had always been aware of my own religious and cultural relativity; but the process of inter-religious and international consultation at the beginning was meant to make this relativity as tolerable as possible. In the declaration I had two concerns.

- Nothing was to be included which could not expect to find a consensus. And a 'cosmic consciousness of unity' presents considerable problems, even in India among Hindus, Sikhs and Muslims. Certainly the cosmos and responsibility for it is constantly present in our Declaration, but 'cosmic consciousness', 'unity of the soul and the universe' could not be generic spiritual nouns in a declaration to which religions of non-Indian origin had to assent.

- In this declaration it was necessary to think through what could be said in common by the great religious traditions for the present situation. Certainly things that were quite incapable of commanding a consensus had to be avoided, but at the same time the consequences of particular ethical maxims had to be expressed clearly and made concrete, even if this was inconvenient for certain religious communities.

The emergence of criticism inside and outside the 'Assembly' was important when one sensed how the individual religious communities were beginning to come to terms with this text intensively. But at the same time it must be said that the controversy was not really at the centre. I was quite delighted to note three things in particular in this discussion.
- No side put in question the need for a Declaration Toward a Global Ethic and its usefulness.
- The basic ethical requirement that 'Every human being must be treated humanely' was accepted as a matter of course (furthermore, it also found a way into the experts' draft of a UNESCO Declaration on Tolerance in Istanbul in April 1993).
- The second complementary basic demand, the Golden Rule, was similarly accepted as a matter of course.

In the draft of the Declaration, from beginning to end I had avoided any quotations of sacred texts: had I not done so there would have been no end to the quotations, because this or that group would have called for a further quotation as a witness from its own tradition on this point or that. But the *Golden Rule* in particular, which is so fundamental, shows impressively that the *common global ethic* of the religions is *not a new invention* but *only a new discovery*. Here again I would like to cite some formulations of the Golden Rule.

- Confucius (c.551-489 BCE): 'What you yourself do not want, do not do to another person' (Sayings 15.23).

- Rabbi Hillel (60 BCE to 10 CE): 'Do not do to others what you would not want them to do to you' (Shabbat 31a).
- Jesus of Nazareth: 'Whatever you want people to do to you, do also to them' (Matt.7.12; Luke 6.31).
- Islam: 'None of you is a believer as long as he does not wish his brother what he wishes himself' (Forty Hadith of an-Nawawi, 13).
- Jainism: 'Human beings should be indifferent to worldly things and treat all creatures in the world as they would want to be treated themselves' (Sutrakritanga I, 11,33).
- Buddhism: 'A state which is not pleasant or enjoyable for me will also not be so for him; and how can I impose on another a state which is not pleasant or enjoyable for me?' (Samyutta Nikaya V, 353.35-342.2).
- Hinduism: 'One should not behave towards others in a way which is unpleasant for oneself: that is the essence of morality' (Mahabharata XIII 114,8).

That brings us to the perspectives for the future.

7. A sign of hope

That such a declaration - and the quality of the signatures should be noted - should in the end have been signed by such significant people as the Dalai Lama and the Cardinal of Chicago, the Vatican representative and the representative of the World Council of Churches, the General Secretary of the World Conference of Religions for Peace and the General Administrator of the International Baha'i Community, the spiritual head of the Sikhs in Amritsar and a president of the Lutheran World Alliance, the patriarch of Cambodian Buddhism, a leading rabbi and an Arab sheikh, represents an unmistakable sign of hope for the future of religions and the peace of the world which beyond question could hardly have been expected only a short time ago.

It will now be an enjoyable task for the scholars of the various religions to work out the project for a global ethic further in the light of their own religions and to bring out three things:
- how strongly the Declaration Toward a Global Ethic is rooted in their own tradition;
- how far their own tradition corresponds with other ethical traditions;
- how far their own tradition has a distinctive, specific, special contribution to make to the ethic.

It need not be repeated that this global ethic should not and cannot strive to be a world ideology or a unitary world religion beyond all existing religions, nor a mixture of all religions. Similarly I should make it clear that even in the future, the global ethic cannot replace, say, the Torah of the Jews, the Christian Sermon on the Mount, the Muslim Qur'an, the Hindu Bhagavadgita, the Discourses of Buddha or the Sayings of Confucius. How could anyone come to think that the different religions wanted to avoid the foundation for their faith and life, thought and actions? These sacred scriptures offer as it were a maximal ethic, compared with which the Declaration Toward a Global Ethic can offer only a minimal ethic. But that does not of course mean an ethical minimalism, though it would already be a great gain if only this minimum of common values, criteria and basic attitudes were realized. What I mean is the minimum of what is now already common to the ethic of the religions of the world and which hopefully can be extended and deepened in the course of the process of communication.

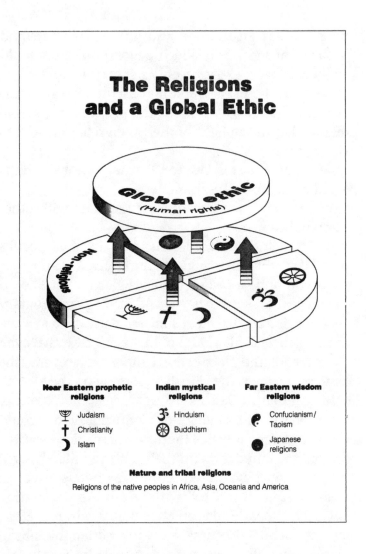

The Religions and a Global Ethic

Global ethic (Human rights)

Non-religions

Near Eastern prophetic religions
- Judaism
- Christianity
- Islam

Indian mystical religions
- Hinduism
- Buddhism

Far Eastern wisdom religions
- Confucianism/ Taoism
- Japanese religions

Nature and tribal religions
Religions of the native peoples in Africa, Asia, Oceania and America

However, the question of a common global ethic is not concerned only with a problem between religions. *Society as a whole is challenged* at a time when after the murder of a two-year-old child by two ten-year-olds now even news magazines like *Der Spiegel* lament in their headlines a crisis of orientation, indeed an *'orientation jungle'* and a removal of tabus without precedent in the history of culture: 'The youngest generation must cope with a confusion of values the extent of which it is difficult to estimate. It can hardly recognize clear criteria for right and wrong, good and evil, of the kind that were still being communicated in the 1950s and 1960s by parents and schools, churches and sometimes even politicians.'[8]

And the editor of the greatest German weekly, *Die Zeit*, Theo Sommer, after the many scandals in politics, business and the trade unions, also appeals to the conscience of the intellectuals: 'The intellectuals of our country must also quite certainly examine themselves. Many of them have preached self-fulfilment to excess; they have mocked virtue, respectability and style; they have for a while taken postmodern arbitrariness so far that in accordance with the slogan "Everything goes", nothing is tabu any more. The criteria are dissolving in the corrosive acid bath of criticism.'[9]

This crisis of orientation is certainly a problem not only for Europe but also for America, and especially also for the area of the former Soviet Union and for China; in other words, it is a global problem.

Are there prospects of a realization of this Declaration? Of course no one knows. It is clear that 'global ethic' has now become a programmatic term and that now a great many people acknowledge particular common principles of a global ethic. But it is also certain that the Declaration Toward a Global Ethic is not yet the realization of a global

8. *Der Spiegel* no.9 ,1993.
9. *Die Zeit*, leading article of 21 May 1993.

ethic. Such a declaration cannot be an end; it can only be the means to an end. And what comes of it will depend on everyone, on you and me.

However, a decisive start has been made. Who in our generation must not concede that he or she did not think as much thirty years ago about nature and the preservation of the natural foundations of life, peace and disarmament, the partnership of men and women, as they do today? A change of global consciousness has taken place in humanity in these three spheres and is constantly expanding. Why should not the same be true of a common ethic for humankind? Surely in thirty years people will think quite differently again about the need for a common ethic for humankind? It should be granted to the younger generation in all the religions on earth, who could then have more orientation, more courage to live and certainly also more true joy in life.

The Parliament of the World's Religions, 1893-1993

Karl-Josef Kuschel

It was to be a triumph of the spirit of modernity: the World Columbian Exposition in Chicago in autumn 1893, held to celebrate the four hundredth anniversary of the 'discovery of America' by Christopher Columbus. For what Hans Küng has called the 'dominant powers of modernity' - science, technology, industry and democracy - came together here in North America at the end of the nineteenth century once again in an impressive way. Here it was once again possible to experience at their peak the achievements of modern times, starting from Europe in the seventeenth century and coming impressively to full development in the United States in the nineteenth century (not least thanks to several waves of European immigration). Here was a demonstration of economics, science and industry on a world scale. Special exhibition palaces had been built to display it which, with their tremendous, striking glass and steel constructions, themselves represented the triumph of the most recent technology.[1]

1. R.H. Seager (ed.), *The Dawn of Religious Pluralism. Voices from the World's Parliament of Religions, 1893*, LaSalle, Illinois 1993.

1. How it all began

One man, *Charles Carroll Bonney*, had a vision which went beyond the material realm. Bonney was a Chicago lawyer and member of the Swedenborgian Church (founded in 1787 and going back to the Swedish scientist and theosophist Emmanuel Swedenborg). He wanted to set something 'higher and nobler' alongside the triumph of the material and the wonder of the technological. Bonney, together with a committee made up of businessmen, pastors and teachers from Chicago, managed to organize a substantial and wide-ranging cultural auxiliary programme to go with the World Exposition ('World's Congress Auxiliary'). There were congresses in all areas of culture from the women's question to social reform, from medicine through the arts to religion. For this purpose yet another special building was erected by the city of Chicago in neo-classical style: the building which now houses one of the most important art museums in the world, the Chicago Art Institute.

For the Department of Religion Bonney secured a pastor of the respected First Presbyterian Church of Chicago, *John Henry Barrows*. Barrows became chairman of a committee which set itself the task of organizing a congress of representatives of the great religions, called The Parliament of World's Religions. From the beginning the committee included the then Catholic Archbishop of Chicago, P.A. Fehan, a subsequently famous Jewish Reform rabbi, Emil Hirsch, fourteen Protestant pastors from Chicago and a Unitarian as General Secretary.

They succeeded in getting forty-five different religions, denominations and organizations to hold their meetings during the World's Congress in Chicago, on the site of the Art Institute which had been provided for this. They also succeeded in getting the greatest attention, the loudest applause and the best press coverage of all the auxiliary exhibitions at the World's Congress. Indeed it must have been a fascinating scene with the representatives of so many religions coming together in one place at the same time, because it was unique.

This also was the strongest expression of what had happened to religion in the course of modernity. It had become - to maintain the imagery - one 'showpiece' among others. More fundamentally, with the modern process of the differentiation of reality into autonomous spheres (beginning with autonomous science and philosophy and the autonomous understanding of the state and politics), religion had lost the position in which it had penetrated and dominated all the spheres of reality, a position which it had still had in the 'paradigms' of the Middle Ages and the Reformation. Now in the modern paradigm it had become a partial sphere of reality, and the Chicago World Exposition merely gave visible symbolic expression to the late consequences of the process of modernity in the sphere of religion.

The initiators themselves had been inspired by others. They were seized with the spirit of *understanding among the nations through the religions*. With the solemnity of the time, in his words of welcome, Charles Carroll Bonney exclaimed: 'This day the sun of a new era of religious peace and progress rises over the world, dispelling the dark clouds of sectarian strife. This day a new flower blooms in the gardens of religious thought, filling the air with its exquisite perfume. This day a new fraternity is born into the world of human progress, to aid in the upbuilding of the kingdom of God in the hearts of men. Era and flower and fraternity bear one name. It is a name which will gladden the hearts of those who worship God and love man in every clime. Those who hear its music joyfully echo it back to sun and flower. *It is the brotherhood of religions.*[2]

And John Henry Barrows enlarged on this at the opening in his own way: 'I believe that the spirit of Paul is here, the zealous missionary of Christ whose courtesy, wisdom, and unbounded tact were manifest when he preached Jesus and the resurrection beneath the shadows of the Parthenon. I believe the spirit of the wise and humane Buddha is here, and of Socrates the searcher after truth, and of Jeremy Taylor and John Milton and Roger Williams and Lessing, the great apostles of toleration. I believe that the spirit of Abraham Lincoln, who sought for a church founded on love for God and man, is not far from us, and the spirit of Tennyson and Whittier and Phillips Brooks, who all looked forward to this Parliament as the realization of a noble idea.'[3]

2. What is a 'parliament' of religions?

The programmatic world 'parliament', parliament 'of religions', which even now causes general amazement and fascination, is also very much in the modern spirit. For as we know, a parliament presupposes democracy, which in turn is a product of the social and political development of modernity. But in 1893 did the religions have a democratic parliamentarian organization and structure? As little then as they do now. At best religions have Synods and World Councils (Protestantism/ Orthodoxy), Electoral Colleges (Catholicism), Assemblies

2. C.C. Bonney, Words of Welcome, in Seager, *Dawn of Religious Pluralism*, 21f.
3. J.H. Barrows, 'Words of Welcome', in ibid., 29f.

(assemblies of rabbis in Judaism and of monks in Buddhism). And many (like Hinduism) do not even have that. But a 'parliament', in the strict sense of a legislative body elected by the people? Not a single religion in the world has one, let alone an institutional world community of religions. But in that case what does 'Parliament of World Religions' mean?

The American Protestant initiators certainly did not envisage the democratic form of a parliament, but a fundamental democratic principle. The 'parliament' was an attempt to express two things:

1. The representatives of the world religions gather together at *the same time in one place*, stand side by side *with equal rights*, and communicate *with respect for one another*. This *de facto* does away with any claim to superiority on the part of one religion over another - at least for the time of the parliament.

2. The representatives of the religions come from the grass roots of their membership, 'from below'. They are not members of the hierarchies of the religions, official delegations sent by their leaders or councils; they represent their religions each in an individual way. So from the beginning the 'Parliament of World Religions' had the *character* not of an institution but *of a movement*, and this guaranteed its dynamic and variety. From the beginning it did not have the character of a statuary diplomatic exchange, but one of spontaneous human *encounter*. Even now its representation is not a matter of official delegation; those involved are personal representatives. Every man and every women represents his or her religion in a unique, irreplaceable way, and is himself or herself an authentic ambassador of his or her own cause.

The parliament has preserved this character of encounter and movement. The second parliament in

1993 was also organized and implemented by a 'Council' of committed men and women supported by a Board of Trustees in which representatives of the religions from the region of the parliament could themselves play a part. Each individual religion was free to take part or not; each was invited to bring representatives from all over the world in order to represent itself. So every religion was itself responsible for the way in which it was to be represented. The success of this parliament thus depended specifically on the question of 'representation' by each individual. The religions were not 'officially' involved, but they were present in so far as thousands of individual representatives reflected the millions upon millions in the religions of the world.

3. A latent 'Anglo-Saxon triumphalism?'

As I indicated, modernity had largely been a product of European history, and in turn was inconceivable without the influence of Christianity. But in 1893 the situation of Christianity was extraordinarily favourable, both politically and socially. Indeed it can be said that at the end of the nineteenth century *Christianity* had 'captured' a *unique position in the world* - and had done so in the course of the colonialist, imperalist, expansionist policy which started from Europe. A combination of Western culture and Christian religion had come to dominate the old centres of culture. India was politically and economically under English control and seemed spiritually exhausted. China was economically, spiritually and politically laid low, the plaything of the European powers. Japan was isolated, Africa colonized. In short, the spirit of modernity was at the same time the spirit of Eurocentrism with a Christian stamp, and this then dominated the world - including North America, to which the Christian Eurocentric world-view had been transplanted in the course of various waves of immigration.

In the 1893 Parliament that had its effect above all on the choice of which groups were invited and which were not. In 1893 those various Christian churches were represented which also played a dominant role elsewhere in the world: Catholicism, Orthodoxy and Protestantism, although the Anglican Church had banned its members from participating.

The significance of the Parliament for *ecumenism within Christianity* cannot be overestimated. In the course of the globalization of European Christian modernity, many people hoped for a unity of the Christian churches. The Parliament was held at a time at which ecumenism within Christianity (which at that time was ecumenism within Protestantism) was beginning to gain a foothold, nurtured by the hope that Christianity would soon establish itself universally as the strongest world religion. So the assessment that the 1893 Parliament was still shaped by a 'strong dose of Anglo-Saxon triumphalism'[4] may also be true.

That was reflected above all by those groups which were either not invited or under-represented. From North America itself, religious communities like the Mormons, or groups excluded from society like the Native Americans, were not represented, nor were the Afro-Americans. But even more significantly, neither Africa nor South America was sufficiently represented (and thus the whole realm of so-called 'tribal religions' was missing). The Muslims were also absent (probably

4. Seager, ibid., 7.

because of a prohibition from the Sultan on taking part in Chicago), as were the Sikhs and the Tibetan Buddhists. Only the ancient Asian religions were represented by significant delegations, which shows that the initiators themselves had no thought of writing off these old religions. Among them two men stood out, who were to become the most significant leaders of modern Hinduism and Buddhism: *Vivekananada*, a young Bengali ascetic, who was to become the leader of Ramakrishna Math, a significant Hindu reform movement; and *Anagarika Dharmapala*, the founder of the Madhi Bodhi Society and leader of a union movement of Buddhist forces in Asia.

This had a concrete effect. In faithfulness to the parliamentary principle of the simultaneous represent-ation and equal rights of all religions, the leaders of the Asian religions for the first time had an opportunity to present their case to the West. Largely still regarded as 'exotic figures', they were able to seize the opportunity to present the wisdom of the religions of Indian origin to a public which was largely imprisoned in a Christianity-centred world view. So we may say with Diana Eck of Harvard University: 'At the time of the Parliament most Americans had never heard the voice of an adherent of the Hindu, Buddhist, or Shinto traditions. European immigration was still in full swing. The exclusion of Asians through a series of immigration acts beginning with the Chinese Exclusion Act of 1882 was a clear statement of the majority view on "American" identity in the United States. Indeed, the nation that hosted the Parliament would not have welcomed its Asian partici-pants as immigrants. One delegate from Japan pointed explicitly to the anti-Japanese sentiment that greeted him in America, with signs that read "No Japanese is allowed to enter here." "If such be the Christian ethics," he said, "well, we are perfectly satisfied to remain heathen."[5]

Thus there can be no doubt that although the 1893 Parliament tried hard to counter a Christanity-centred world view; although its initiators were concerned to demonstrate the plurality of religions with equal rights and equal status within one humankind; and although the spirit of progress, optimism and understanding between the nations might prevail in the heads of the participants, the turn of the century was not yet the time for really coming to terms with the plurality of the religions. On the contrary, in their hearts the Christian churches still hoped that they would be the beneficiaries of the process of modernity. For with the globalization and universalization of technology, economics and industry, Christianity seemed to have the best prospects of establishing itself as a universal religion.

Moreover, what the Christian churches really thought does not become clear in the 1893 Parliament of World's Religions. To discover that we have to look at the World Missionary Conference of Protestant missionary societies which took place in Scotland seventeen years later, in 1910, in Edinburgh. Here ecumenism within Christianity had found its first visible expression. Still inspired by the triumph of Christian countries like Great Britain (and in its wake the United States), the Edinburgh Conference saw Christianity as having a unique historical opportunity. In almost apocalyptic language they enthused about the 'uniqueness of the historical moment', which lay in the fact that the Christianization of the whole world could be expected within a space of only ten years. 'Our survey has impressed on us the momentous

5. D. Eck, 'Foreword', in Seager, *Dawn of Religious Pluralism*, xvi.

character of the present hour. We have heard from many quarters of the awakening of great nations, of the opening of long-closed doors, and of movements which are placing all at once before the church a new world to be won for Christ. The next ten years will in all probability constitute a turning point in human history, and may be of more critical importance in determining the spiritual evolution of mankind than many centuries of ordinary experience. If those years are wasted, havoc may be wrought that centuries are not able to repair. On the other hand, if they are rightly used, they may be among the most glorious in Christian history... There is an imperative spiritual demand that national life and influence as a whole be Christianized: so that the entire impact, commercial and political, now of the West upon the East, and now of the stronger races upon the weaker, may confirm, and not impair, the message of the missionary enterprise. The providence of God has led us all into a new world of opportunity, of danger, and of duty.'[6]

4. The collapse of Eurocentric Christian modernity

Nineteen years after the first Parliament of Religions and only four years after the Edinburgh Conference, the First World War had broken out, and the position of the Christian Great Powers (above all Germany and Great Britain) had been deeply shaken. The Second World War saw to the rest. What seemed to have been conquered and exhausted revived and began to change world history all over again:

6. *The History and Record of the World Missionary Conference. Edinburgh 1910*, Vol.9, Edinburgh 1910, 108-9.

- With the revolution in *China* (beginning in 1911 under Sun Yat-Sen and ending after a long civil war with the proclamation of the People's Republic under Mao-tse-tung in 1949) a corrupt and spiritually rotten feudal system had been swept away. China's strength increased particularly after the Second World War, and with it also the Chinese tradition, which (at first still under anti-religious Communist control) was also to set free its religious forces. There are tangible signs of this.

- In the course of the non-violent liberation movement under Mahatma Gandhi, in 1947 *India* gained its independence from Great Britain. And with the strengthening of the state, the influence of *Hindu culture and religion* also increased worldwide, especially in North America and Europe. In particular, this was because with Reform Hindus like Ramakrishna and his pupil Vivekananda in the nineteenth century and Radhakrishnan and Sri Aurobindo in the twentieth, India had significant thinkers who aimed at an influence far beyond India.

- In the course of the Zionist immigration movement into Palestine, in 1948 *Israel* succeeded in founding an independent state under David Ben Gurion. Thus almost nineteen centuries after the destruction of the Second Temple (by the Romans in the year 70 CE), Judaism again had a central focus. And with this centre Judaism also became stronger as a religion, especially as significant thinkers like Martin Buber, Franz Rosenzweig, Abraham Heschel and Joseph Soloveitchik had been able to translate the old message of Yahweh and his people for modern times.

- At the latest after the oil crisis at the beginning of the 1970s the world public had become aware of the social power of *the Arab states shaped by Islam*. And at the latest from the end of the Shah's regime in Iran, the world public was shown at a stroke by one of the most important leaders of Shi'ite Islam that *Islam as a religion* was still in a position to write world political history. Moreover the increase in the political and economic power of lands under Islamic influence meant a strengthening of Islam as a religion (particularly in Africa, but also in Europe and North America). One special factor here was the way in which social contrasts in the individual Islamic countries fed, and still feed, fundamentalist opposition groups. Islam, too, can point to significant reformers in the course of the nineteenth and twentieth centuries who succeeded in translating the message of the Qur'an communicated by the Prophet Muhammad for a new time and thus demonstrating the capacity of Islam for spiritual change. Among them, in the India of the nine-teenth century, were Sayyid Ahmad Khan and after him the spiritual father of Pakistan, the poet-philosopher Muhammad Iqbal; but mention should also be made of the charismatic father of a modern Islam focussed on reform in the Middle East, Jamaladdin al-Afghani.

What follows from this development? That the expectations of Christianity that it would become *the* dominant universal world religion in the twentieth century, in the wake of Eurocentric modernity, failed all along the line. Not only was the world not Christianized; on the contrary, at the end of the twentieth century on the whole the other religions of humankind are stronger than they were at the beginning. The world-view of Euro-centric Christian modernity has been replaced.

In his *Global Responsibility* Hans Küng has shown that with the First World War the modern world generally had to accept a decisive break. The modern world order was replaced *by a 'postmodern' world order* ('postmodern' is a makeshift heuristic term which initially was meant simply to describe experiences different from those of modernity). Postmodernity has the following factors (here I am merely recalling remarks made in this connection in *Global Responsibility*):

- Already at that time it was clear to many people that the world domination of the European powers had been fundamentally shattered and that after this global political earthquake Eurocentricism had been replaced by a *polycentrism* (not only Europe but now America, Soviet Russia and also Japan).

- Already at that time it had become clear that modern science and technology would give wars an essentially different *quality of annihilation* and that a new war with an even more perfect technology of death could completely ruin Europe.

- Already at that time there was a *peace movement* which argued resolutely for total disarmament or even pacifism.

- Already at that time there was a massive *criticism of civilization*, and those who were far-sighted had seen that industrialization would not only bring technical progress but in time would also destroy the environment.

- Already at that time the *women's movement* in many countries had achieved its definitive breakthrough: equal rights in political elections and in the choice of profession began to become established.

- Already at that time the *ecumenical movement* began, with international conferences and alliances; after the Second World War it was to lead to the World Council of Churches and the Second Vatican Council.

For the religious situation of humankind in the post-modern paradigm, in principle this means:

- No more attempts by one religion to push aside other religions by aggressive mission strategies, and no more arrogant and triumphalist lording it of one religion over others;

- But also no subtle triumphalistic efforts by other religions to transcend themselves in attempts at a universal or even syncretistic mixing, with the aim of forming a single world religion from all the other religions;

- Rather, the peaceful co-existence and pro-existence of the various religions in mutual respect, in dialogue and collaboration.

It goes without saying that in the face of a world which is increasingly more closely bound together by communication technology, economically and financially interdependent, and mutually dependent ecologically, such talk is idealistic. Countless men and women in all religions pursue this ideal, but by no means all. Day by day it is quite evident that in numerous regions of this earth the religions are still incapable of pursuing or unwilling to pursue the ideal of mutual respect, dialogue and collaboration. The scenes of this refusal are generally known:

- In *Northern Ireland*, Catholics and Protestants still carry on bloody and murderous feuds.

- In *Bosnia-Herzegovina*, Christians (the Croatian Catholics and the Serbian Orthodox) and Muslims (Bosnians) are caught up in a bloody civil war which has now already cost thousands of dead, tens of thousand of wounded and hundreds of thousands of refugees and homeless.

- In *India*, in the Punjab and Kashmir, Hindus and Sikhs, Hindus and Muslims, are engaged in bloody clashes over sanctuaries, mosques and temples, which month by month cost dozens of lives.

- In *Sri Lanka*, Hindus and Buddhists are entangled in ethnic conflicts, incapable of overcoming the limits of their own tribal allegiances (Singhalese and Tamils) in the spirit of religious understanding.

- In the *Middle East* Jews and Muslims are so dominated by their respective fanatics that the laboriously negotiated, sensational first peace agreement between Israelis and Palestinians (September 1993) seems again constantly to be in danger. And even if the questions of a state and borders are one day settled by treaty, it will presumably take generations for the prejudices and feelings of hatred to disappear from the hearts of people on both sides.

And yet, in the face of the manifold tensions and wars which have also been inspired and legitimated by religion, who could dispute that, to quote the slogan of the inspiration of the first World Parliament of Religions, Charles Carroll Bonney, there is no alternative to the 'brotherhood of religions'? A century after the first Parliament this statement is a programme which is not yet out of date, indeed is more urgently necessary than ever. Why?

5. The polyreligious situation of our time: Chicago as an example

What the initiators of the first World Parliament presumably did not even dream of has come about in the course of this century: the world has grown together and at the same time the religions of the earth have also come closer together. That is particularly unmistakable in the major cities of North America and Europe. For after the American Congress removed its restrictions on immigration for people from Asia, men and women came into the major American cities from Asian countries and of course also brought their religions with them. Once they had achieved economic prosperity, in the

91

1970s and 1980s they also began to give outwardly visible expression to their religion: Buddhist monasteries, Indian ashrams, Sikh temples and Muslim mosques arose. And anyone who travels through the great metropolises of the United States and Canada (whether New York or Toronto, Vancouver or Los Angeles) encounters this phenomenon. A largely monocultural society with a European Christian stamp has been replaced by a multi-cultural, multi-religious society.

According to the most recent figures the *religious situation in the United States* is as follows: 44% of the population are Protestants, 26% Catholics, 1% Orthodox Christians, 2-3% Jews and 3% Mormons. 9% describe themselves simply as 'Christians' or belong to one of the many sects or inter-confessional churches outside the traditional confessional camp. 2% of the population of the United States belong to religions outside the Jewish-Christian tradition, i.e. are adherents of Islam, Buddhism or Hinduism. Their number is increasing.[7]

But these are abstract percentages. They immediately become more eloquent if one gives the figures about individual groups, both nationwide and as reflected in a megalopolis like Chicago:[8]
- Whereas in 1893 adherents of Buddhism like Anagarika Dharmapala were still looked on with amazement at the first World Parliament as exotic figures, in the United States *Buddhism* today numbers four million followers, 155,000 of them in Chicago alone. Twenty-eight different Buddhist organizations are present here, which embrace

7. I have taken these figures from the most recent report in the *National Catholic Reporter*, 10 September 1993.
8. I have taken the following figures from the report in the *Chicago Tribune Magazine*, 29 August 1993.

all branches of Buddhism: Tibetan, Japanese and Vietnamese Buddhism along with Korean and Thai Buddhism. In addition there are 1500 American converts. - Whereas the Hindu delegation led by Swami Vivekananda was still regarded as a sensation at the first World Parliament, *Hindus* today can count a million adherents in the United States, 100,000 of them in the Chicago area alone. Here members of this faith community have a dozen temples.

- Whereas precisely one adherent of *Jainism* (an Indian religion of non-violence going back to Mahavira, who proclaimed it in the fifth century BCE, so that it arose at the same time as Buddhism) succeeded in taking part in the first World Parliament, today there are already 70,000 adherents of Jainism in the United States, 2,500 of them in Chicago alone; they have just succeeded in building a temple here.

- Whereas in 1893 the *Muslims*, too, were represented by a single delegate (a convert from Anglicanism), today there are already 250,000 Muslims in Greater Chicago, who have given expression to their religion by building numerous mosques.

- Whereas *Zoroastrians* were absent from the First World Parliament, in the United States today estimates put the adherents of Zoroastrianism at 10,000, 500 of them in Chicago, where they have their own Zoroastrian centre.

What is true of Chicago is also true of other major cities, especially in the highly industrialized Western world. As in a microcosm, these world cities reflect the opportunities and problems of the macrocosm. So it was no coincidence that the initiative for a second Parliament of the World's Religions again came from a megalopolis like Chicago. For the question how such different and mutually contradictory religions can live together in one city or world community is today more urgent than ever before. Since the religions no longer exist separated from one other in distant continents, but very close together, questions of inter-religious co-operation and capacity for dialogue arise afresh. This time, however, they no longer do so against a modern background (with the subtle or direct expectation of the domination of one religion), but against a postmodern background. If the first Parliament of the World's Religions was dominated by modernity, the second is dominated by postmodernity. If the first was dominated by a universal ideal of the 'brotherhood of religions', the second had to occupy itself with concrete questions of the coexistence of the religions and thus with questions of common convictions, values, basic attitudes: in short, with questions of an ethic common to all religions.

6. Conflicts and opportunities in the 1993 Parliament

The awareness of living in a changed historical era was reflected in the second Parliament in the spectrum of groups which this time were present or fully represented: not only Muslims and Zoroastrians, Jains and Tibetan Buddhists, but above all 'native Americans' and a broad spectrum of the most varied cults, spiritual groups and religious movements. Who in particular took part in the Parliament emerges best from the opening and closing plenaries, the programmes of which we have included as an appendix in the documentation section of this book.

Generally speaking, it can be said that even in outward appearance the classical religions did not take first place, but the varied religious groups and groupings (a high priest of Isis was particularly spectacular here). By their dress, ceremonies and presentation of themselves the latter attracted attention which was often in inverse proportion to their true significance. But under the cover of the Parliament they made better use of the opportunities to draw attention to themselves and their concern than others did. Be this as it may, the 'Council' of the Parliament was well advised to admit such groups, although in so doing it provided ammunition for the traditional Christian churches, who from the start disqualified such a Parliament as syncretistic. Moreover there was immediately a first conflict over such 'neo-pagan' groups. This and other conflicts must be mentioned briefly to give a realistic picture of the second Parliament.

1. Even at the planning stage, *evangelical and fundamentalist church groups* refused to collaborate in the Parliament. This antipathy to inter-religious activities was doubtless also fed by the fact that a 'neo-pagan' group was allowed to hold a moon ceremony in Chicago's Grant Park. The group of the *Greek Orthodox of Chicago* took this as an occasion to break off their participation in the congress completely (though in any case it was so small as to be almost non-existent). However, this did not prevent the Syrian Orthodox Metropolitan Mar Gregorios from India from taking part in the sessions of the 'Assembly' of delegates.

2. During the Parliament *four Jewish groups* withdrew their support. They were protesting against the presence of Louis H. Farrakhan of the 'Islamic Nation', which they described as 'antisemitic', and therefore rejected. However, this did not prevent important representatives of Judaism from continuing their work in the Parliament constructively.

3. When in a speech a citizen of *Kashmir* condemned as 'psychological rape' the fate of his land, divided

between India, Pakistan and China, and the loss of his culture and his holy places, he was shouted down by a number of Indians in the audience. Tumult followed.

4. The *'Declaration Toward a Global Ethic'* worked out and presented by Hans Küng on behalf of the Council provoked vigorous discussions. As was only to be expected, some people questioned the procedure itself (the text, which had gone through a long process of consultation, could not be changed futher); others had doubts about its content (above all about the equal place given to men and women, the question of non-violence and the character of the document as a whole, which was thought to be 'too Western'). Indeed the proposal was made that this declaration should be demoted to the status of a 'Working Paper', to water down its binding quality. However, this was rejected. At the end of a tedious process of discussion an overwhelming majority of delegates supported the text without change, once it had been termed an 'Initial Document Toward a Global Ethic'. In his contribution to this book Hans Küng has commented on all this at length.

However, these conflicts did not harm the cause of the Parliament. On the contrary, it became clear that this Parliament was not being held outside our earth in a space ship - in an atmosphere of artifically contrived harmony - but in the middle of this world. It was therefore a reflection of what is actually taking place in the world; a microcosm which reflects the macrocosm. 6,500 participants were offered around 700 individual events. These consisted, first, of a broad range of purely religious events (inter-religious ceremonies, meditations) presented by individual religions, and secondly, of a broad range of major presentations, individual lectures, seminars, workshops, dialogue groups and inter-religious training programmes, aimed at making it possible to experience inter-religious learning and inter-religious encounter in practice.

Of course it is impossible to report everything that went on among the thousands of participants during the Parliament. However, the predominant impression seemed to be that this Parliament offered a unique occasion to get to know people of another faith, to exchange views with them, to hear of the problems of others at first hand and to report one's own. In this way countless threads of dialogue were woven together. A vast amount of information was exchanged, meetings were made possible, prejudices demolished. There was not an elevator trip in which one was not asked where one came from, or could ask where other participants came from; not a meal at which people did not immediately get to the point in their conversation; not a lecture in which one was not entangled in a discussion of one's faith background. Anyone who wanted to learn about inter-religious activity had abundant opportunity here. And we all went away richly rewarded. Without exaggeration it can be said that anyone who went to Chicago and spent seven full days there returned home a changed person.

7. The main themes: Global thinking - spirituality - ethics

The awareness of living in a changed historical era was also reflected in the *dominance of themes characteristic of postmodernity*. It is worthwhile again recalling the key-words: polycentrism, war and peace, a critique of civilization, the women's movement, the ecumenical movement. Similarly, already in his *Global Responsibility*

Hans Küng had brought out the criticism of Western achievements from Asia and Africa, achievements which had established themselves in European modernity. They had made many great contributions to the world, not just good ones:

- *Science, but no wisdom* to prevent the misuse of scientific research.
- *Technology, but no spiritual energy* to bring the unforseeable risks of a highly-efficient macrotechnology under control.
- *Industry, but no ecology* which might fight against the constantly expanding economy.
- *Democracy, but no morality* which could work against the massive interests of various individuals and groups in power.

This in particular was also reflected in *the main speeches to the Parliament*. Here I can give extracts from only four of them, by Gerald O. Barney, Robert Muller, Hans Küng and the Dalai Lama.

Right at the beginning of the Parliament *Dr Gerald O. Barney* shook his audience with an impressive speech on the social, economic and ecological state of our globe. As early as the 1970s, at the request of President Jimmy Carter, Barney and his Millennium Institute had presented a major report with the title *Global 2000*. Now he presented a revised version brought up to date with the most recent information: *Global 2000 Revisited*. With precise statistics and graphics Barney illustrated the most urgent problems: waste of land, population growth, food production, energy reserves, ecological pollution, the hole in the ozone layer ...

From this he concluded. We need an *interdependent, networked thought*. The idea of the 'sovereignty' of modern nation states is false. 'Nations are not independent entities subject to no other power on Earth. They are all interdependent and very much subject to the health and welfare of the entire ecosystem of Earth, of which they are but a modest part. The imaginary lines around nations, the "borders", generally have no relationship to the boundaries of watersheds, airsheds, and other natural systems and complicate the development of mutually enhancing Earth-human relationships. The rules (laws) nations establish to govern human and institutional behaviour within their borders are generally based on the assumption that the non-human part of Earth is simply a "resource" of no value until "used" by humans.'.[9]

People might also already have heard or read some of this elsewhere. In terms of information it was not particularly new, though that is not meant to deny the significance of Barney's impressive analyses and appeals. But what was new was that Barney also brought into his analyses the role of religions in coping with the tasks facing the world. Here he began from the correct insight that the religions of the world now exercise an important influence on the conduct of millions of people. To exclude them in an analysis of social, economic and ecological problems, as was often done in the past, would be to ignore a decisive factor.

So Barney was well advised to remind the religions critically of their responsibility for world peace and the

9. G.O. Barney, *Global 2000 Revisited. What Shall We Do?*, Arlington, Virginia 1993, 64.

ecosystem: 'The religions of the world will have a powerful influence on the human future. Currently there are about forty wars in progress around the world, and the hostilities inspired by religions are major factors in virtually every one of these wars. Religious beliefs also stand in the way of attention to a number of critical issues. The best known of many examples is the attitude of various faiths to family planning, but equally important are teachings concerning "progress" and the difference between needs and wants. For these reasons it is critically important that the leaders of the world's religions be engaged in a dialogue on the critical issues of the future.'[10]

The speech by *Dr Robert Muller*, Chancellor of the Peace University established by UNO in Costa Rica, who was Deputy General Secretary of the United Nations in the 1950s and 1960s, also went in the same direction. He too called for a *dialogue between politics and religion,* between *science and spirituality.* He too was convinced that while we may have technology at our disposal, we have not discovered our 'spiritual energies'. He pinned all his hopes on these human 'spiritual energies'. Spirituality was the key word, and he opposed it to a social, economic and ecological fatalism: 'What science, politics, economics and sociology were trying to achieve, the religions knew long ago by virtue of transcendence, elevated consciousness and union with the universe and time. This dimension is still missing, yet it is urgently needed in world affairs.'[11]

10. Ibid., 90.
11. Parts of Muller's speech had been published in advance in J.Beversluis, *A Sourcebook for the Community of Religions,* Chicago, Illinois 1993, IX.

In a very personal speech influenced by his own religious experiences, Muller therefore passionately pleaded for a 'world cathedral of spirituality and religions'. He quoted the remark of the atheist André Malraux, that either the third millennium will be 'spiritual' or there will be no third millennium. And with Dag Hammarskjöld, one of the most charismatic General Secretaries of the United Nations, he expressed his conviction: 'I see no hope for permanent world peace. We have tried and failed miserably. Unless the world has a spiritual rebirth, civilization is doomed.'[12]

For Muller this *spiritual rebirth* was all-important. It was here that he saw the decisive role of the religions all over the world. With the solemnity of a man who had spent forty years in the service of the United Nations and nevertheless had not given up hope of a new humane civilization, he appealed to his audience: 'Religions and spiritual traditions: the world needs you very much! You, more than anyone else, have experience, wisdom, insights and feeling for the miracle of life, of the Earth, and of the universe. After having been pushed aside in many fields of human endeavour, you must again be the lighthouse, the guides, the prophets and messengers of the one and last mysteries of the universe and eternity. You must set up the mechanisms to agree, and you must give humanity the divine or cosmic rules for our behaviour on this planet.'[13]

Hans Küng took up the same basic notion with less pathos and more sober analysis in his speech about the need for ethical rules for human behaviour on this planet. The method and hermeneutic of the Declaration

12. Ibid.
13. Ibid., ixf.

Toward a Global Ethic that he outlined and completed after a complex process of communication need not be explained again here, since Hans Küng has already written about it in his chapter, but its connection with the general themes of the Parliament should be stressed here once again. For what Gerald O. Barney and Robert Muller called for was also Küng's concern. The force of religious convictions must be applied to overcome the global problems of humankind. But this can happen only if the religions stop wearing one another down in disputes, fomenting conflicts and preaching fanaticism, and reflect on what is common to them. If they do that, the power of the religions would benefit all humankind. For this power lies in their capacity literally to transcend the sphere of laws, precepts and institutions. The religions can address men and women at quite other depths: not merely at the levels of rational calculation, of operations and strategies, but at the level of the heart, the feelings, the 'soul'.

One might also add that the fact that an overwhelming majority of the delegates from all religions signed the Declaration Toward a Global Ethic and were not deterred from this by the controversies in the discussions shows that among the far-sighted in all religions a process of consciousness has come about over the challenges of postmodernity. No religion any longer exists in splendid isolation. There is a widespread awareness that people are dependent on one another and need mutual respect, dialogue and collaboration for the well-being of humankind as a whole. And this is all the more urgent, since fanaticism in the ranks of religion has increased considerably in the last fifteen years.

This is true of all religions. All must try to damp down the 'spirits' of hatred and enmity again before they get completely out of control. Here all the leaders of all religions have a common task, indeed a common responsibility. Here the call for mutual respect, dialogue and collaboration is not a 'Western import' but is itself grounded in the sources of the individual religions themselves. The very acceptance of the Declaration Toward a Global Ethic shows that in an impressive way: evidently in all religions there are ethical traditions, values, criteria and norms which contribute to such a declaration. Anyone who signed such a declaration had not fallen for a refined 'Christian' take-over strategy, the victim of a subtle Western cultural imperialism, but was rather convinced that the contents of this declaration could also be advocated equally by Jews, Muslims, Hindus, Buddhists, Sikhs or Zoroastrians. Indeed the skill in the composition of this declaration consisted in its formulation of an ethic in such a way that anyone could recognize themselves in it from their own tradition. So those of us who had come from Tübingen listened with great satisfaction to the report of the executive director of the Parliament, Dr Daniel Gómez-Ibáñez. He told us about a Buddhist delegate who, when he had read the declaration, had signed it spontaneously with the remark, 'Here I hear the voice of the Buddha.' A rabbi whom we met in turn felt reminded of the Decalogue.

The voice of the Buddha could also be heard in an impressive way in the speech by the *Dalai Lama*. As a Nobel Peace Prize winner he had been invited to give the main address at the closing meeting of the Parliament on 4 September in the open air in Grant Park, Chicago. The content of the Dalai Lama's speech, too, was not really of great originality. One has already heard him talk often of understanding between peoples, mutual respect between religions, respect for the different paths to the one Absolute. One has already heard him plead often for human rights, human dignity, respect for life, respect for creation, without in so doing omitting critical questions like family planning and population growth. So too it was in Chicago.

Something else seems decisive to me: authenticity and humanity. The reason why the Dalai Lama's speech was so convincing, and indeed seized people's hearts, so that it was often interrupted by spontaneous applause, was that this man simply wanted to be an *authentic Buddhist*. His plea for mutual respect, dialogue and collaboration, for understanding between peoples and respect for creation, was not an adaptation to Christian or Western values but came from the depths of his own Buddhist spirituality. As a Buddhist, as a disciple of Buddha Gautama, this great leader of Tibetan Buddhism called on people to overcome all fanaticism and all conflicts and come together in love.

The same thing is true of the Dalai Lama's *humanity*. He did not convince people through rhetorical brilliance but through humour, a smile and a deep warmth which gripped his audience. At no point did one get the impression that here a refined tribune of the people knew the craft of mass manipulation, that here the magisterium was preaching from above. On the contrary, what the Dalai Lama said came from the heart and went to the heart. His humanity was an authentic humanity formed by Buddhist spirituality. The humanity of a disciple of Buddha! But this was a humanity which this Buddhist at the same time attributed to the disciples of the Prophet, the disciples of Jesus Christ, the disciples of Moses and all the many other religious leaders or founders on this earth.

So the Parliament had key moments which at the same time will be starting points for the future:[14] the passing of the Declaration Toward a Global Ethic and the address by the Dalai Lama late that same afternoon of 4 September 1993. The Declaration Toward a Global Ethic for the first time gives a signal that representatives of the religions, with good will, are capable of publicly emphasizing binding values, irrevocable criteria and concrete norms and canvassing for a capacity for peace, a readiness for dialogue and collaboration among their adherents. This hope is bound up with the fact that a broad process of growing ethical consciousness is beginning in individual religions and strengthening all the forces which are now working towards this goal. The address by the Dalai Lama similarly points structurally towards the future: every religion is called on to mobilize in itself ethical traditions and spiritual sources which will contribute to the well-being of humanity as a whole. These are ethical traditions and spiritual sources which support what is stated in the introduction to the Declaration Toward a Global Ethic: 'We are inter-dependent. Each of us depends on the well-being of the whole, and so we have respect for the community of living beings, for people, animals, and plants, and for the preservation of Earth, the air, water and soil. We take individual responsibility for all we do.'

14. Cf. the extremely informative account by Marcus Bray-brooke, *Pilgrimage of Hope. One Hundred Years of Global Interfaith Dialogue*, London and New York 1992. This encouraging book traces the effect of the first Parliament (pp. 5-42) on the subsequent movement for understanding between the religions.

Documentation

A. The Opening Plenary of the Parliament

Saturday, 28 August 1993
Grand Ballroom of the Palmer House Hilton, Chicago

1. Procession of the Delegations

Musical Accompaniment by Drepung Loseling Monks
'Invocation of the Forces of Goodness'

Sri Lanka Theravada Buddhist

Cambodian Buddhist

Wat Dhammaran Thai
(with Ven. Achalin Chuen Phangcham)

*

Buddhist Women's Network

Buddhist Society of Compassionate Wisdom

The World Fellowship of Buddhists

Numara Center for Buddhist Research

Rissho-Kosei-Kai

Buddhist Churches of America

Won Buddhist United Nations Office

Buddhist Host Committee
(with Rev. Gyomay Kubose)

*

Baha'i Host Committee
(with Dr Wilma Ellis)

*

Federation of Jain Associations in North America

Institute of Jainology

International Mahavir Jain Mission

Jain Society of Metropolitan Chicago

Anmivrat Society

Jain Host Committee
(with His Highness Suskil Kumar Ji Maharaj)

*

Dharmadhatu Meditation Center

Gelugpa Vajrayana
(with Ven. Samdhong Rinpoche)

*

Brahma Kumaris
(with Ven. Sister Pratima)

*

Dharma of Chicago

Sri Annaramacharya Project of North America

Vishwa Hindu Parishad

Hindu Temple of Greater Chicago

Hindu Host Committee
(with Swami Chidananda)

*

Sikh Dharma International

Gobind Sadan USA

Guru Gobind Singh Foundation

Sikh Host Committee
(with Bhai Mohinder Singh)

*

Kwan Um School of Zen

Korean Zen

Zen Bultasa

Chung Tho Mission Center

Kyoto School (with Professor Masao Abe)

*

Jabala Society

Sri Chinmoy (with Dr Kapila Castoldi)

*

Vivekananda Vedanta Society
(with Swami Ghahananda)

*

International Society of Divine Love
(with Hari Dasi)

*

United Church of Christ Chicago Midwest

1st United Church of Oak Park

1st Presbyterian Church of Lake Forest

4th Presbyterian Church

Presbyterian Church USA

National Council of the Churches of Christ in the USA

World Alliance of Reformed Churches

Protestant Host Committee

North II Conference United Methodist Church
(with Bishop R. Sheldon Ducker)

Evangelical Lutheran Church
(with Rev. Carl McKenzie)

*

Episcopalian Host Committee
(with Bishop Frank Griswold)

*

Swedenborg School of Religion

Church of New Jerusalem: Swedenborgian
(with Rev. David Roth)

*

National Council of Christians and Jews

Spertus College of Judaica
(with Dr Howard Sulkin)

*

Focolare

St Isidore Church

St John De La Salle Church

Catholic Theological Union

De Paul University

Monastic Interreligious Dialogue

The Archdiocese of Chicago
(with Joseph Cardinal Bernadin)

*

Covenant of the Goddess

Earth Spirit Community

Center Women, the Earth, the Divine

Yoruba

Circle Sanctuary

Lyceum of Venus of Healing

The Fellowship of Isis
(with Lady Olivia Robertson)

*

Taoist Tai Chi Center of Canada
(with Eva Wong)

*

Islamic Research Foundation

American Islamic College

Muslim Host Committee
(with Dr Irfan Khan)

*

Greek Orthodox Diocese

Orthodox Church of America
(with Bishop Job)

*

Anthroposophical Society in America

International Church of Metaphysics

Liberal Catholic Church

The Theosophical Society

The Theosophical Society in North America
(with Dr John Algers)

*

Shinto
(with Professor Tadahiro Ohnuma)

*

City of God
(with Paramahamsa Krishna Swami)

*

Association of Rastafarian Theologians

Illinois Conference of Churches

Evanston Ecumenical Action Council

Science of Spirituality

Self-Realization Fellowship

Hyde Park and Kenwood Interfaith Council

International Association of Religious Freedom

Unity and Diversity World Council

Interreligious Federation for World Peace

The Organization of Universal Communal Harmony (TOUCH)

Fellowship of Prayer, Inc

Women of Faith (with Ms Gretchen Leppke)

*

New Covenant Missionary Baptist Church

Forever Gospel

African-American Protestant Host Committee
(with Dr Leon Finney)

*

Attending Marshals:
Br Gregory Perron, OSB

Ms Jossie Seelund

Mr Erik Larson

*

Federation of Zoroastrian Associations of North America

Zoroastrian Host Committee
(with Dastoor Kobad Zarolia)

*

Council for a Parliament of the World's Religions

Trustees and Dignitaries:
Dr Nelvia Brady

Mrs Betty Reneker

Dr Daniel Gómez-Ibáñez

Dr David Ramage

Mayor Richard M. Daley, Chicago

Governor Jim Edgar, State of Illinois

*

Native American Indian Center Madison

Native American Community of Chicago

Native American Host Committee
(with Elder Oren Lyons, Elder Alfred Yazzie, Elder Thomas
Banyacya, Elder Ernest Pigeon, Elder Thomas Yellowtail)

*

Processional Marshal
Rev. Julian von Düerbeck, OSB, KGCA

*

1st Unitarian Universalist Church of Ann Arbor

Unitarian Universalist Association Council Midwest District
(with Rev. Tony Larsen)

*

North American Conference of Christians and Ecology

Ribbon International

American Academy of Childcare and Family Services

Greater Chicago Broadcasting Ministries

The Center for Yoga and Christianity

Religions Education Association

Universal Peace Sanctuary

World Conference on Religion and Peace

Millennium Institute

Sserulania Foundation

Joseph Campbell Foundation
(with John Lobell)

*

Attending Marshals
Mrs Vakil Wilkinsen
Mr Brian P. Pace

II. The Ceremony

Introduction
Mayor Richard M. Daley, Honorary Chairperson

Governor Jim Edgar

Meditation

Welcome
Dr Daniel Gómez-Ibáñez
Executive Director
Council for a Parliament of the World's Religions

Invocations
American Buddhist Congress
Venerable Dr Chuen Phangcham

Archdiocese of Chicago
Cardinal Joseph Bernadin

Spiritual Assembly of Baha'i
Dr Wilma Ellis

Brahma Kumaris
Sister Pratima

Sikh Host Committee
Bhai Mohinder Singh

Hindu Host Committee
Swami Chidananda

United Methodist Church
Bishop R.Sheldon Duecker

American Islamic College
Dr Irfan Khan

119

Greek Orthodox Diocese
Bishop Job

Spertus College of Judaica
Dr Howard Sulkin

Opening of the Parliament
Dr David Ramage
Chairperson Board of Trustees
Council for a Parliament of the World's Religions

Presentation

Blessings from Four Directions and Center
Native American Elders

East Oren Lyons

South Alfred Yazzie

West Thomas Banyacya

North Thomas Yellowtail

Center Ernest Pigeon

Introduction to Blessings
Dr Nelvia Brady

Blessings
Vivekananda Vedanta Society
Swami Ghahanananda

Evangelical Lutheran Church
Rev. Carl McKenzie

Unitarian Universalist
Rev. Tony Larsen

Fellowship of Isis
Lady Olivia Robertson

Church of New Jerusalem: Swedenborgian
Rev David Roth

Theosophical Society in America
Dr John Algeo

Federation of Zoroastrians
Dastoor Kobad Zarolia

Buddhist Council of the Midwest
Rev. Gyomay Kubose

Closing Remarks
Mrs Betty Reneker

B. The Closing Plenary of the Parliament

Saturday, 4 September 1993
Grant Park, Chicago

I. Procession of the Delegations

Musical Accompaniment by Drepung Loseling Monks

'Prayer for World Peace'
'Dedication of Creative Energy'

Marshals
Mr Erik Larson, Mr Kashf-i-Nur Heine and Mrs Vakil Wilkinsen

225 Spiritual Assembly Members

14 Task Force Members

41 Trustee Members

Stage Procession
Mrs Eva Hochgraf, MDiv
Dignitary Marshal

Mr Brian P. Pace
Attending Marshal

Mr Joseph E. Perry
Attending Marshal

32 Dignitaries

Rev. Julian von Duerbeck, OSB, KGCA
Processional Marshal

II. The Ceremony

Introduction
Dr Daniel Gómez-Ibáñez
Executive Director
Council for a Parliament of the World's Religions

Report from the Assembly of Delegates
Dr David Ramage
Chairperson of the Board of Trustees
Council for a Parliament of the World's Religions

'The Declaration Toward a Global Ethic'

Proclamation of the Short Version

Report from the Metropolitan Assembly of Religions in Chicago
Dr Jeffrey Carlson (De Paul University)

Introduction of Council for a Parliament of the World's Religions
Trustees
Dr Leon Finney

Introduction to Invocations
Ms Yael Wurmfeld

Invocations from Dignitaries and Presidents

Multi-cultural Dance Performance
Introduction:
Omi Baldwin, Native American Elder

'A Call for Peace Drum and Dance Company'
Native American, East Indian, Mung, African, Irish, Middle Eastern, Jewish, Aztec

Choir Performance
Chicago Soul Children's Choir
Mr Walt Whitman, Director

'God Is'
by Robert Freyson

'O Lord We Praise Thee'
by Hezekiah Walker

Concluding Farewell
Dr David Ramage

Exit
Dignitaries and Trustees
(musical accompaniment by the Chicago Soul Children's
Choir)

'Exhortation of Praise'
by Robert Freyson